Basic Arabic

by Kathrin Fietz

English Edition by

Mohamed A. Alsiadi
Rutgers University, New York University

Arif M. Rana
Rutgers University, Brookdale Community College

Course Book

Berlitz Publishing
New York   Munich   Singapore

NO part of this book may be reproduced, stored in a retrieval system or transmitted in any form or means electronic, mechanical, photocopying, recording or otherwise, without prior written permission from Apa Publications.

Contacting the Editors
Every effort has been made to provide accurate information in this publication, but changes are inevitable. The publisher cannot be responsible for any resulting loss, inconvenience or injury. We would appreciate it if readers would call our attention to any errors or outdated information by contacting Berlitz Publishing, 193 Morris Avenue, Springfield, NJ 07081, USA. Fax: 1-908-206-1103, email: comments@berlitzbooks.com

All Rights Reserved
© 2009 Berlitz Publishing/APA Publications GmbH & Co. Verlag KG, Singapore Branch, Singapore

Original Edition: 2007 by Langenscheidt KG, Berlin and Munich
Printed in China, December 2009

Berlitz Trademark Reg. U.S. Patent Office and other countries. Marca Registrada. Used under license from Berlitz Investment Corporation

Cover photos © Mark Karrass/Corbis

Publishing Director: Sheryl Olinksy Borg
Editor/Project Manager: Nela Navarro
Arabic Language Consultant: Arif M. Rana
Cover design: Elizabeth Gaynor
Interior art: Ute Weber
Production Manager: Elizabeth Gaynor

Table of Contents

How to Use This Course 4

Scope & Sequence 6

Pre-Lesson 7

Lesson 1 21

Lesson 2 31

Lesson 3 41

Lesson 4 52

Test 1 63

Lesson 5 65

Lesson 6 75

Lesson 7 86

Lesson 8 96

Lesson 9 108

Test 2 119

English Translation of Dialogues 121

Listening & Speaking Exercises 125

Answer Key: Lessons 133

Answer Key: Tests 138

Glossary 139

How to Use This Course

Welcome! Congratulations on your decision to learn Arabic. This practical course will help you to acquire the necessary tools to accomplish this goal, whether your focus is vocabulary, grammar, or pronunciation. To master the four key elements of a language—listening, speaking, reading, and writing—a variety of exercises to practice these skills have been included in this course.

Classical Arabic, the language of classical Arabic literature is complex. Since Classical Arabic use it is not used in conversational speech, in this course we focus on Modern Standard Arabic (MSA), and colloquial Arabic. We present practical vocabulary, expressions and basic grammar as they are used in the Arabic-speaking world.

To manage everyday Arabic, you will learn the most common words and expressions and the grammatical structures of written and spoken Arabic. We'll also provide you with additional information about regional linguistic differences and colloquial usage in Egypt and Syria. We chose these dialects specifically because they are commonly understood in all of the Arabic-speaking world.

Because you decided to learn Arabic on your own, without a teacher, each lesson is divided into sections with clear instructions and explanations including many helpful examples and learning tips. The following paragraphs explain how the book is structured and how to use it in the most effective way.

Lesson Structure

Every lesson follows the same pattern:
On the first page, next to the lesson number, there is a box that illustrates the learning goals of that lesson. In addition, there is usually one reading, accompanied by a translation. These short readings are taken from everyday life in Arabic countries and relate to the topic of the lesson.

The section **What's new?** explains the grammatical focus of the lesson using examples from the first text.

The main section of each lesson consists of a dialogue, which will help familiarize you with spoken Arabic. These dialogues appear on CD 1 of this course. Here you can listen to the rhythm and melody of the Arabic language, first in Standard Arabic, then the Syrian and Egyptian dialects. The translations of the dialogues are in the back of the book.

The **Vocabulary** list contains the relevant dialogue's vocabulary words and their translations which appear in the dialogue and the reading. We added the phonetics to help you with the pronunciation. Simply read it as it were English, noting any special rules.

The **Grammar** section introduces new grammar step by step. But you don't have to go through the entire grammar section before you do the exercises; The yellow arrow tells you which exercises go with which grammar points. For additional grammar review and reference go to www.berlitzbooks.com/basicarabic.

In the **Usage** section, you'll learn how to apply Arabic in everyday situations. Be sure to practice the idioms and expressions! You'll impress your new acquaintances and friends during your travels to Arabic-speaking countries.

Under **More Useful Expressions** you'll find additional vocabulary and phrases that are relevant to the topic of the lesson. Try to memorize them.

In **Regional Variations** you will find the Syrian and Egyptian equivalents of some Standard Arabic expressions. Although you don't have to memorize these variations, they will help you understand the dialogues you will hear on CD 1.

Exercises appear at the end of each lesson. These exercises help you practice what you have learned. You can check your answers in the answer key at the end of the book. Remember that the exercise can be easily completed by going back and reviewing the dialogues, vocabulary or grammar sections in the lesson. Please note that the answers in the answer key appear in Arabic script to encourage you to recognize Arabic script. You can however write your answers using the phonetic system that we provide for you. We do encourage you to try to write your answers in script as well. We also encourage you to practice recognizing script.

In Culture Note/Language Note

You will find important and interesting language and culture information related to the topic of the lesson.

Tests

You'll find a **Test** after lesson four and another one after lesson nine. The tests are designed to give you an opportunity to assess what you've learned. All the major points of the previous lessons are included here. If you do well on the test by getting a majority of correct answers, you are ready to move to the next lesson. Your total points and the answers can be found in the answer key at the end of the book.

How to Work with the Book

Here is a basic guideline for studying: Try not to do too much at a time. Instead, try to work with the material a ideally on a daily basis or several times a week for about 30 minutes without interruption. Before you start with the first lesson familiarize yourself with the Arabic script, alphabet, and pronunciation. Write the letters and words several times and listen to the sounds on the CD 1.

Are you ready for the first lesson?
Read the text first. Don't be intimidated by the new words. It's more important to see what the text is about than to understand every word. The dialogue, the main component in each lesson, takes you into the world of the spoken language. Here, language comes to life. We suggest you listen to the dialogue once or twice without the book. Make notes of what you do understand: words, phrases, parts of sentences. If you do not understand focus on the sounds and listen again. To make it a little easier, we recorded the dialogues at two different speeds. It might also help you to break up the dialogue in smaller sections.

Finally, listen to the entire dialogue again, this time reading along with the book. If you feel that you understand the dialogue, after using the vocabulary section or the translation, read it out aloud. Try to act out what the people are saying. Don't be afraid to sound silly. Immerse yourself completely into the sounds and rhythm of the language. In order to remember all those new words and expressions, it may help you to write them down. A time-tested method is to use flashcards, notes or your own vocabulary database.

Listening & Speaking CDs (CD 2 and CD 3)

Two of the audio CDs (CD 2 and CD3) included in the program contain exercises that will improve your listening and speaking skills. The exercises and the tasks associated with them are in the **Listening and Speaking** section of your book, and they are linked to the topic of each lesson. The correct answers for the exercises are in the answer key at www.berlitz.com/basicarabic.

Although you will find the instructions to each exercise in the book, the audio CD will give you more detailed information about the task and will provide you with examples. At times you'll be asked to simply listen. At other times you will be asked to listen and repeat, answer orally, write answers in the book, or read along with the book. Therefore, for some exercises, you'll need the book, but since this section is about your listening comprehension and speaking skills, try to do the other exercises without the book. If you need help, go to the answer key section.

Abbreviations

adv	adverb	*islam*	Islamic
alt	alternatively	*lit*	literally
app	appropriately	*loc*	locally
Arab	Arabic	*m*	masculine
coll	collective	*MSA*	Modern Standard Arabic
Egy	Egyptian	*o.s.*	oneself
Eng	English	*pl*	plural
ex	example	*sl*	slang/informal
f	feminine	*s.o.*	someone
fre	French	*s.th.*	something
geo	geographically	*Syr*	Syrian
imp	imperative		

Scope & Sequence

Text		Topics	Grammar
Pre-Lesson			
Intro **Reading** Map: The Arab World	العالم العربي	Arabic-speaking countries **Language and Culture Note:** Words from the Quran	Arabic Script, alphabet, pronunciation Articles Numbers 0–10
1 **Reading** Passports **Dialogue** أهلاً وسهلاً!	مصري وسورية	Greetings and introductions Nationalities Saying good bye **Culture Note:** Saying hello	Adjective ending *nisba* Personal pronouns Simple sentences with *to be* Demonstrative pronouns
2 **Reading** Hotel Brochure **Dialogue** بكم الغرفة؟	مرحباً بكم في فندق الباشا!	Accommodations Booking a hotel room Making polite requests	Suffixes The verb *to have* Singular, dual, plural Word structures
3 **Reading** City Map **Dialogue** جديد في المدينة	خريطة المدينة	Downtown/The Center of town Asking for directions Describing routes and locations	Adjectives Numbers 11–100 Numbers with nouns
4 **Reading** Road Signs **Dialogue** إلىٰ مركز المدينة	إشارات المرور	Means of transportation Locations Small talk on the road Time expressions **Culture Note:** Taking a taxi	Genitive constructions Simple negative sentences Sentences with كان
5 **Reading** A Letter **Dialogue** علىٰ التليفون	رسالة من القاهرة	Asking for the time of the day Telling time Days of the week Meeting with someone **Culture Note:** The weekend	The past tense Question word *what* in a sentence The Accusative
6 **Reading** Film Trailer **Dialogue** في مقهىٰ أبو سعيد	فيلم مصري	Family status Occupations Telling age Idioms with الله (God) **Culture Note:** Family life	The present and future tenses Adverbs
7 **Reading** Advertisements **Dialogue** في السوق	محل للشرقيات	Going shopping Colors Making apologies **Culture Note:** Currencies	Verbs with prepositions Prices, suffixes with prepositions Imperative… Numbers 100–1000
8 **Reading** Cooking Recipe **Dialogue** في المطعم	سلطة تبولة	At the restaurant Groceries Expressing likes and dislikes **Culture Note:** Paying at a restaurant	Verb stems Suffixes with verbs Negative sentences Collective nouns
9 **Reading** Greeting Card **Dialogue** رمضان كريم!	عيد مبارك!	Family members Introductions Giving congratulations **Culture Note:** Islamic holidays	Stem IV Weak verbs Indirect speech

Pre-Lesson

In this lesson you will learn:
- The Arabic Script
- Pronunciation in Arabic-Speaking Countries
- Numbers 0–10

The Arab World العالم العربي

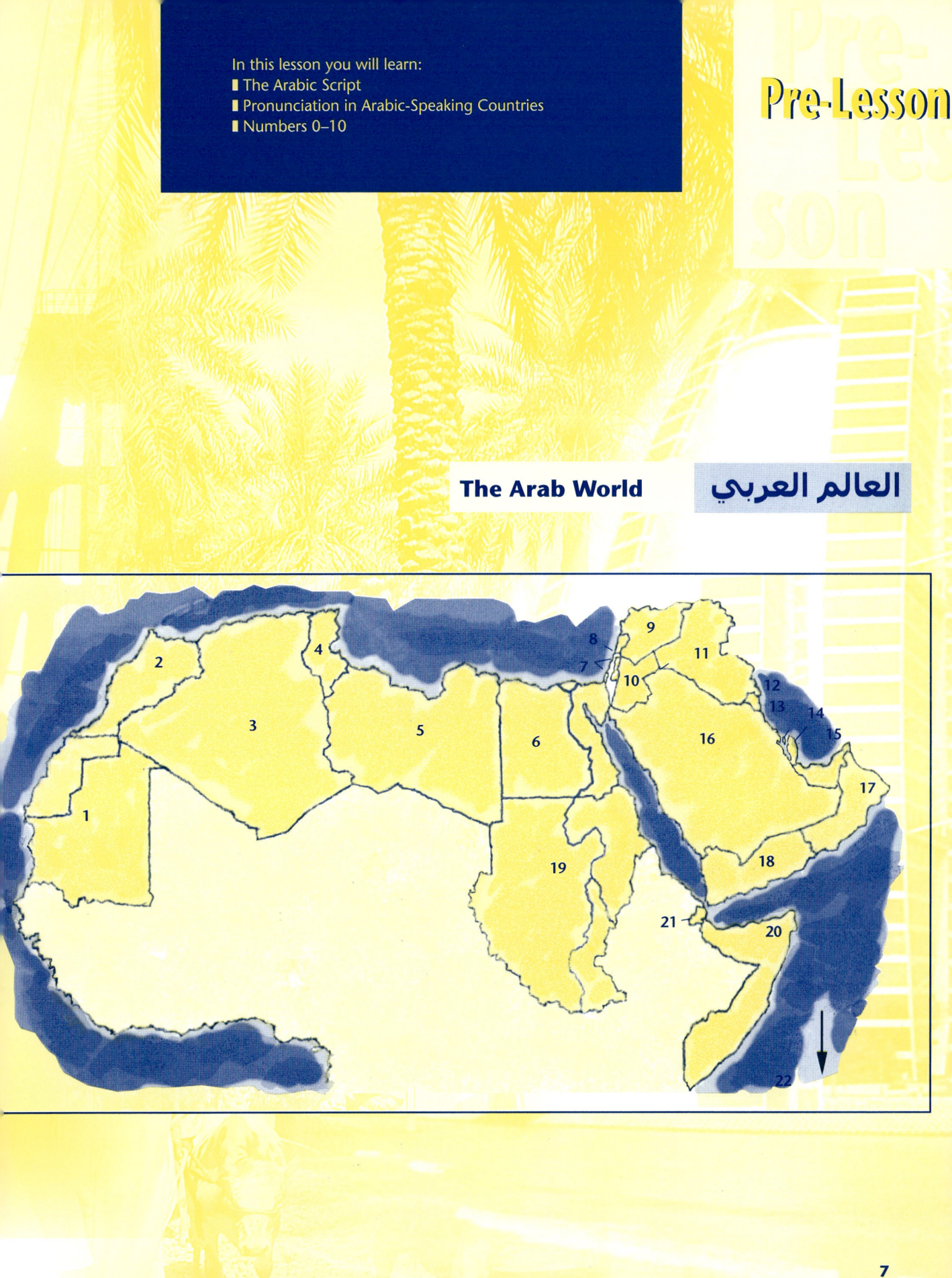

المفردات

The Arabic-speaking world is classified into three large geographical regions, the West المَغْرِب [al-maghrib], the East المَشْرِق [al-mashriq], and the Arabian Peninsula الجَزيرة [al-jazeerah], which includes the Gulf region الخَليج [al-khaleej]. The following are member states of the Arab League, and their official language is Arabic: 1

1	Mauritania	mooreetaanyaa	مُوريتانيا
2	Morocco	al-maghrib	المَغْرِب
3	Algeria	al-jazaa'ir	الجَزائر
4	Tunisia	toonis	تونِس
5	Libya	leebiyaa	ليبيا
6	Egypt	miSr	مِصْر
7	Palestine	filasTeen	فِلَسْطين
8	Lebanon	lubnaan	لُبنان
9	Syria	sooriyaa	سوريا
10	Jordan	al-urdunn	الأُرْدُنّ
11	Iraq	al-'iraaq	العِراق
12	Kuwait	al-kuwayt	الكُوَيْت
13	Bahrain	al-baHrayn	البَحْرَين
14	Qatar	qaTar	قَطَر
15	United Arab Emirates (UAE)	al-imaaraat	الإمارات
16	Saudi Arabia	as-sa'oodeeyah	السَّعوديّة
17	Oman	'umaan	عُمان
18	Yemen	al-yaman	اليَمَن
19	Sudan	as-sudaan	السّودان
20	Somalia	aS-Soomaal	الصّومال
21	Djibouti	jeebootee	جيبوتي
22	Comoros	juzur al-qumur	جُزُر القُمُر

The Arabic Script

The Arabic alphabet consists of twenty-eight letters. Arabic is written from right to left (except the numbers). All letters (except six) are connected with each other to make words. There are spaces between words and there is no capitalization and there are no hyphens.

In order to practice writing Arabic letters most effectively, write down each letter in a notebook following the examples in this lesson. Always start from the right hand side, keeping your pencil on the page until the end of the word or a letter that is not connected before adding the appropriate dots.

List of Letters

Final Form	Medial Form	Initial Form	Sound Produced	Name	Letter
ا	ا	ا	ʾ / aa	ʾalif(*)	ا أ إ
ب	ب	ب	b	baaʾ	ب
ت	ت	ت	t	taaʾ	ت
ث	ث	ث	th (1)	thaaʾ	ث
ج	ج	ج	j	jeem	ج
ح	ح	ح	H	Haaʾ	ح
خ	خ	خ	kh	khaaʾ	خ
د	د	د	d	Daal(*)	د
ذ	ذ	ذ	th (2)	thaal(*)	ذ
ر	ر	ر	r	raaʾ(*)	ر
ز	ز	ز	z	zaay(*)	ز
س	س	س	s	seen	س
ش	ش	ش	sh	sheen	ش
ص	ص	ص	S	Saad	ص
ض	ض	ض	D	Daad	ض
ط	ط	ط	T	Taaʾ	ط
ظ	ظ	ظ	TH (3)	THaaʾ	ظ
ع	ع	ع	ʿ	ʿayn	ع
غ	غ	غ	gh	ghayn	غ

Pre-Lesson

Letter	Name	Sound Produced	Initial Form	Medial Form	Final Form
ف	faa'	f	ف	ف	ف
ق	qaaf	q	ق	ق	ق
ك	kaaf	k	ك	ك	ك
ل	laam	l	ل	ل	ل
م	meem	m	م	م	م
ن	noon	n	ن	ن	ن
ه	haa'	h	ه	ه	ه
و	waaw(*)	w / oo	و	و	و
ي	yaa'	y / ee	ي	ي	ي
ء	hamza	'	أ إ	ـﺄ	ئ ؤ ء

(*) Letter is not connected to the letter that follows.

(1) frontal <u>th</u> as in "<u>th</u>anks"

(2) medial <u>th</u> as in "mo<u>th</u>er"

(3) medial <u>th</u> as in "mo<u>th</u>er" but more emphatic

Short Vowels and Letter Marks   7

Fatha [a] a little diagonal slash above the letter, identifies a short *a* as in the word *fallafel*. Double slashes above an alif identify the ending [- an].

| under | taHt | تَحْت |
| very | jiddan | جِدّاً |

Kasra [i] identifies a short *i* as in *fit*. It is written as a little diagonal slash under the letter.

| headscarf/covering | Hijaab | حِجاب |

Damma [u] identifies a short oo-sound, as in *foot*. It is written as a little "9" above the letter.

| love | Hubb | حُبّ |

Sukun tells us that the consonant is not followed by a vowel as in the word *props*. It is written as a little circle above the letter.

| sister | ukht | أُخْت |

Shadda doubles a letter. They are pronounced or spoken twice but not written twice. It is written as a little "w" above the letter. Fatha and damma are placed above the "w", kasra below the "w".

| I love/like | uHibb | أُحِبّ |
| she loved/liked | aHabbat | أَحَبّت |

Long Vowels

For the three corresponding short vowels you have just studied, there are three long vowels. Ironically, three consonants in the Arabic language also function as long vowels. The consonant 'alif [ا] when used as a long vowel produces the "aa" sound. The consonant waaw [و] when used as a long vowel produces the "oo" sound. Finally, the consonant yaa' [ي] when used as a long vowel produces the "ee" sound.

القواعد

The Letters 6

The Arabic alphabet consists of letters for consonants. There are also three short vowels which are written above or below the letter they follow. However, they are normally not shown in most Arabic texts as the reader is expected to know them. Long vowels and diphthongs are created by making a combination of the short vowels and the letters **alif** [ا], **waaw** [و], and **yaa** [ي].

Because letters are connected with each other, each letter changes its shape depending on whether it is at the beginning, in the middle, or at the end of a word. Below, from right to left, each letter is shown in three ways. It is first shown individually, then the beginning, middle, and end. The six letters which are not connected are shown as individual/beginning and middle/end variations. They are also marked (*).

Stress
Stress in words is usually even or falls on long vowels, for example, a word like **yameen** has the stress on the long vowel (aa), while a word like **laban** would be pronounces with equal stress on both syllables.

1. 'alif (*)
[', aa] As a consonant, the 'alif does not have a sound of its own. However, when used as a long vowel, it produces the long "aa" sound, as in the English word, f**a**r. This letter is not connected to a letter that follows it.

end	middle	beginning	individual
ــا	ــا	ا	ا

Below you find each letter along with an explanation of the pronunciation. You will also see an example word.

2. baa'
[b] **b** as in the word **b**at.

end	middle	beginning	individual
ـب	ـبـ	بـ	ب

door   [baab]   باب

3. taa'
[t] **t** is pronounced like the **t** in the word **t**ea.

end	middle	beginning	individual
ـت	ـتـ	تـ	ت

to stay overnight   [baat]   بات

4. thaa'
[th] **th** is pronounced like the **th** in the word **th**anks. (Modern Standard Arabic)

Pre-Lesson

end	middle	beginning	individual
ـث	ـثـ	ثـ	ث

furniture   [athaath]   أثاث

5. jiim
[j] It is pronounced like the **j** in the word **j**am.

end	middle	beginning	individual
ـج	ـجـ	جـ	ج

answers   [ijaabaat]   إجابات

6. Haa'
[H] It is pronounced with a strong, breathy **h** like the **h** in **h**appiness.

end	middle	beginning	individual
ـح	ـحـ	حـ	ح

researcher   [baaHith]   باحث

7. khaa'
[kh] There is no real equivalent in English. The **h** sound comes from the back of the throat as in the word Ba**ch**.

end	middle	beginning	individual
ـخ	ـخـ	خـ	خ

brother   [akh]   أخ

8. daal (*)
[d] **d** as in the English word **d**ad. This letter is not connected to a letter that follows it.

end	middle	beginning	individual
ـد	ـد	د	د

chicken   [dajaaj]   دَجاج

9. thaal (*)
[th] **th** as in the word mo**th**er. Like daal, this letter is not connected to a letter that follows it.

end	middle	beginning	individual
ـذ	ـذ	ذ	ذ

Take! (m)   [khuth]   خُذ!

10. raa' (*)
[r] **r** as in the word **r**ain. This letter is not connected to a letter that follows it.

end	middle	beginning	individual
ـر	ـر	ر	ر

news   [akhbaar]   أَخْبار

Pre-Lesson

11. zaa' (*)
[z] **z** as in the word **z**ebra. Again, this letter is not connected to a letter that follows it.

end	middle	beginning	individual
ـز	ـز	ز	ز

bread   [khubz]   خُبْز

12. seen
[s] **s** as in the word **s**un.

end	middle	beginning	individual
ـس	ـسـ	سـ	س

lesson   [dars]   دَرْس

13. sheen
[sh] **sh** as in the word **sh**ut.

end	middle	beginning	individual
ـش	ـشـ	شـ	ش

to drink (lit he drank)   [sharib]   شَرِب

14. Saad
[S] This is prounounced with a strong, emphatic **s**.

end	middle	beginning	individual
ـص	ـصـ	صـ	ص

Morning   [SabaaH]   صَباح

15. Daad
[D] This is prounounced with a strong, emphatic **d**.

end	middle	beginning	individual
ـض	ـضـ	ضـ	ض

green   [akhDar]   أَخْضَر

Culture and Language Note

Daad is very important in the Arabic language. Arabic is considered the language of the **Daad**. In school and when the Quran is read of, particular emphasis is put on the correct pronunciation of **Daad**. Depending on the region, the differences between Daad (15), THaa' (17), and thaal (9) may be hardly audible.

16. THaa'
[T] Is pronounced with a strong, emphatic **t** as in the word **t**oast.

end	middle	beginning	individual
ط	ـطـ	طـ	ط

Potatoes   [baTaaTaa]   بَطاطا

Pre-Lesson

17. THaa'
[TH] The letter THaa' is a heavy version of thaal, (the letter 9).

end	middle	beginning	individual
ظ	ظ	ظ	ظ

luck   [HaTHTH]   حَظّ

18. 'Ayn
['] A guttural sound made by tightening the throat.

end	middle	beginning	individual
ـع	ـعـ	عـ	ع

Arabs   ['arab]   عَرَب

19. ghayn
[gh] like the French **r**, as in **r**ue or like a gargling sound.

end	middle	beginning	individual
ـغ	ـغـ	غـ	غ

West, occident   [gharb]   غَرْب

20. faa'
[f] **f** as in the word **f**an.

end	middle	beginning	individual
ـف	ـفـ	فـ	ف

apples   [tuffaaH]   تُفَّاح

21. qaaf
[q] the **q** sound is pronounced from the back of throat, sometimes dropped in spoken Arabic.

end	middle	beginning	individual
ـق	ـقـ	قـ	ق

East, orient   [sharq]   شَرْق

22. kaaf
[k] **k** as in the word **k**art.

end	middle	beginning	individual
ـك	ـكـ	كـ	ك

thanks   [shukran]   شُكْراً

23. laam
[l] **l** as in the word **l**ip.

end	middle	beginning	individual
ـل	ـلـ	لـ	ل

man   [rajul]   رَجُل

If laam is followed by an alif, both letters form a ligature or a double letter. Subsequent letters are not connected with an alif.

لا

ـلا

no   [laa]   لا

Culture and Language Note

In Arabic [allaah] God, laam is pronounced **ll** as in the English word ba**ll**. The small alif indicates that laam is followed by a long [aa]. This little alif, called the dagger alif, is also used in other words from the Holy Quran [al-qur'aan], e.g. in [ar-raHmaan], the Merciful, one of the 99 names of God in Arabic.

24. meem
[m] **m** as in the word **m**an.

end	middle	beginning	individual
ـم	ـمـ	مـ	م

peace   [salaam]   سَلام

25. noon
[n] **n** as in the word **n**ever.

end	middle	beginning	individual
ـن	ـنـ	نـ	ن

we   [naHnu]   نَحْنُ

26. haa
[h] slightly aspirated **h** as in the word **h**ouse.

end	middle	beginning	individual
ـه	ـهـ	هـ	ه

hello   [ahlan]   أَهْلاً

Taa' Marbuta: Feminine Ending

The ending of a feminine word produces an **ah** sound as in the word algebr**a**.

language   [lughah]   لُغَة   ـة   ة

27. waaw (*)
[w, oo] Waaw can be pronounced in two ways first, [w] **w** as in the word **w**in and then [oo], **oo** as in the word f**oo**d. If it preceded by a fatha, it becomes the diphthong **au** [au] as in the word **au**to. This letter is not connected to a letter that follows it.

end / middle	beginning / individual
ـو	و

coffee   [qahwah]   قَهْوَة

Pre-Lesson

light	[noor]	نور
excursion	[jawlah]	جَوْلَة

In some cases, hamza (29) sits on top of yaa' or waaw. It serves as an auxiliary on "helping" letter and doesn't have its own sound.

question	[soo'aal]	سُؤَال

28. yaa'

[y, ee] Yaa' can also be prounounced in two different ways, **[y] y** as in the word **y**et, and **[ee], ee** as in English f**ee**t. If it preceded by a fatha, it becomes the diphthong **ay [ay]** as in English s**ay**. In some cases, hamza (29) sits on top of yaa'. It serves as an auxiliary or "helping" letter and doesn't have its own sound.

end	middle	beginning	individual
ـي	ـيـ	يـ	ي

in	[fee]	فِي
house, apartment	[bayt]	بَيْت

In some cases, hamza (29) sits on top of yaa' or waaw. It serves as an auxiliary or "helping" letter and doesn't have its own sound.

questions	[as'ilah]	أَسْئِلة

A yaa' without the two dots is called an Alif Maksoora. The Alif Maksoora produces the **[aa]** sound and is pronounced like **a** in the word c**a**r.

to	[ilaa]	إِلىٰ

29. hamza

['] Hamza signifies a glottal stop. It sounds like the sound you make when you drop the **tt** in *butter* (*bu'er*).

end	middle	beginning	individual
ئ ؤ ء	ئـ	أ إ	ء

father	[ab]	أب

When an alif is followed by another alif with a hamza you add an accent mark called a *madda*.

fathers	[aabaa']	آباء

Light and Heavy sounds in Arabic

Having studied all the consonants of the Arabic alphabet, it is important to note that the Arabic language has 6 light sounds that have a corresponding heavy sounds:

ك	س	ذ	د	ه	ت	ا	Light sound
k	s	th	d	h	t	'	
ق	ص	ظ	ض	ح	ط	ع	Heavy sound
q	s	TH	D	H	T	'	

It is very important for you to differentiate the respective sounds. Failure to do so would result in the change of meaning. See examples below:

كُل [kul] = all/each   قُل [qul] = say (command)!

طين [Teen] = mud   تين [teen] = fig

Letters producing heavy sounds appear as caplitalized letters in the English transliteration.

Article

There is only one article in Arabic, ال [al-]. It is always written alongside the noun. In Arabic there is no equivalent of the indefinite article *a / an*.

a house, an apartment   [bayt]   بَيْت

the house, the apartment   [al-bayt]   البَيْت

The alif of the article is generally connected to the preceding vowel.

in the house / apartment   [fee l-bayt]   في البيت

More on Pronunciation with Articles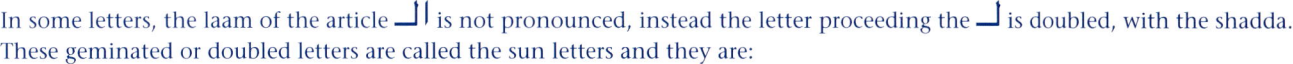

In some letters, the laam of the article ال is not pronounced, instead the letter proceeding the ل is doubled, with the shadda. These geminated or doubled letters are called the sun letters and they are:

ن   ل   ظ   ط   ض   ص   ش   س   ز   ر   ذ   د   ث   ت

| *the sun* | [ash-shams] | الشَّمْس | *the man* | [ar-rajul] | الرَّجُل |
| *the peace* | [as-salaam] | السَّلام | *the light* | [an-noor] | النّور |

With all other letters, the laam of the article is fully pronounced. These letters are called the moon letters and they are:

ي   و   ه   م   ك   ق   ف   غ   ع   خ   ح   ج   ب   ا

| *the moon* | [al-qamar] | القَمَر | *the West* | [al-gharb] | الغَرْب |
| *the news* | [al-akhbaar] | الأَخْبار | *the Arabs* | [al-ʿarab] | العَرَب |

Spelling

Although the Arabic language has punctuation marks, there are no binding rules. Note the differences between the comma in English (,) and the question mark (?).
Words that consist of only one letter, like the conjunction و [wa] *and*, never appear by themselves. They are always connected to the word that follows.

the East and the West	[ash-sharq wa-l-gharb]	الشَّرْق وَ الْغَرْب

Aside from the ligature lam-alif (see page 16) other letters can form connections to ensure a more fluent writing style, e.g.

		Ligature	Basic Form
the love	al-Hubb	الحبّ	الـحبّ
we	naHnu	نحن	نـحن
Muhammad	muHammad	محمّد	مـحمّد
pretty	jameel	جميل	جـميل
good	tamaam	تمام	تـمام

More Useful Words

عبارات مفيدة أخرى

In English we use Arabic numerals. In Arabic speaking countries, especially in the Middle East and the Arabic Peninsular, Indian numericals are used. Numbers greater than 9 are written and spoken from left to right.

٠	zero	Sifr	صِفر	٦	six	sittah	سِتّة
١	one	waaHid	واحِد	٧	seven	sab'ah	سَبعة
٢	two	ithnayn	إثنَين	٨	eight	thamaaniyah	ثَمانية
٣	three	thalaathah	ثلاثة	٩	nine	tis'ah	تِسعة
٤	four	arba'ah	أَربَعة	١٠	ten	'asharah	عَشَرة
٥	five	khamsah	خَمسة				

Regional Variations

في العامية

Although written Modern Standard Arabic (MSA) is identical in all Arabic speaking countries, there are considerable differences in pronunciation and accents among the different countries. For example

▌The letter thaa' (4) is pronounced as a soft [t] in many Arabic dialects.

two	[itnayn]	إتْنَين

▌The letter jeem is pronounced in Syria [j], in Egypt [g] and in Lebanon [3].

pretty	[jameel/gameel/3ameel]	جَميل

Pre-Lesson

■ The letter qaaf is pronounced in some countries like the sound of **q** as in the word [q], in Cairo and Damascus like hamza, and in Jordan and the Gulf region like [g] as in the English word **g**olf.

coffee   [qahwah/'ahwah/gahwah]   قَهْوة

■ The pronunciation of short vowels can vary from country to country.

Palestine   [falasTeen/filasTeen]   فِلَسْطين ، فَلَسْطين

Exercises   التمارين

1 Connect the pronunciation to the appropriate script of these nationalities as shown in the example. Then go to the first page of this lesson and find the countries on the map. Answer the exercises by using the phonetic spelling you see in the lesson.

a. [miSr]   1. الأردنّ
b. [al-'iraaq]   2. المغرب
c. [al-maghrib]   3. عمان
d. [al-urdunn]   4. سوريا
e. [sooriyaa]   5. العراق
f. ['umaan]   6. مصر

2 Write the dates in English as shown in the example.

.... ١٩٥١ 5.   .... ١٩٦٣ 3.   2007 ٢٠٠٧ 1.
.... ١٦٤٣ 6.   .... ١٩٨٥ 4.   .... ١٩٩٩ 2.

3 Mark in which instances the lam of the article is <u>not</u> pronounced. The first one has already been done for you.

☐ البحرين 5.   ☐ السودان 3.   ☒ السعودية 1.
☐ الشمس 6.   ☐ النور 4.   ☐ الجزائر 2.

4 Write the words with the articles.

.... صباح 5.   .... خبز 3.   ..الدرس..... درس 1.
.... سلام 6.   .... أخبار 4.   .... بيت 2.

19

Pre-Lesson

5 Connect the letters to form words as shown in the example.

.. باب ......   1. ب + ا + ب
....   2. س + ل + ا + م
....   3. و + ا + ح + د
....   4. ص + ب + ا + ح
....   5. أ + ل + م + ا + ن + ي + ا
....   6. ا + ل + إ + م + ا + ر + ا + ت

6 Which six letters are not connected with the letter that follows?

.... 6.   .... 5.   .... 4.   .... 3.   .... 2.   .... 1.

7 Add the appropriate letter marks as in the example.

[lughag]   لـغـة   5.   [jawlah]   جـولـة   3.   [shukran]   شُكْراً   1.

[uHibb]   أحـب   6.   [ahlan]   أهـلا   4.   [ilaa]   إلـى   2.

الدرس الأول ١

In this lesson you will learn:
- **Personal information**
- **Greetings and saying good bye**
- **Nisba adjectives**
- **Personal pronouns**
- **Simple sentences with** *to be*
- **Simple sentences with** *this is/these are*

مصريّ وسوريّة
An Egyptian and a Syrian

الاسم: كريم عبد الرحمٰن محمّد
الجنسية: مصري
تاريخ الميلاد: ١٣ / ١٠ / ١٩٦٥
مكان الميلاد: القاهرة

Name: Kareem Abd ArRahmaan Muhammad
Nationality: Egyptian
Date of Birth: 13-10-1965
Place of Birth: Cairo

الاسم: فاطمة حلّاق
الجنسية: سورية
تاريخ الميلاد: ١٤ / ١٢ / ١٩٧٨
مكان الميلاد: دمشق

Name: Faatimah Hallaq
Nationality: Syrian
Date of Birth: 14-12-1978
Place of Birth: Damascus

Language Note

Like most Arabic texts, the dialogues and texts in this book are not vocalized except in cases where it is not clear what is meant. The vocabulary lists and examples contain words with characters. Fatha, kasra, and damma were not used where a long vowel is marked by alif, yaa, or waaw. Try to avoid character. Instead try to memorize the script visually and the pronunciation.

What's New? ما الجديد؟

What's new? In the Pre-Lesson you have already learned about the taa' marbuta (ة), the ending of almost all feminine nouns and adjectives. There are few exceptions (e.g., أُمَ [umm] *mother*). They are identified with the letter *f* in the glossary. All other words are masculine.

The Nisba Ending 3

A Nisba is the transformation of a noun (person, place, thing) into an adjective (word describing a noun). Nationalities (adjectives) are created by using the name of the country (noun) without the article and feminine taa' marbuta (ة), and adding the Nisba ending ـِي [-ee] or ـِيَّة [-eeyah].

masculine			feminine		
Egyptian	miSree	مِصْري	Egyptian	miSreeyah	مِصْريَّة
Syrian	sooree	سوري	Syrian	sooreeyah	سوريَّة
Jordanian	urdunneeyah	أُرْدُني	Jordanian	urdunneeyah	أُرْدُنِيَّة

Here are the names of the countries from which the adjectives in the chart above were formed:

Egypt	miSr	مِصْر	Syria	sooriyaa	سوريا	Jordan	al-urdunn	الأُرْدُنّ

ahlan wa sahlan أهلاً وسهلاً !

Thomas has been learning Arabic for a while. In the street he runs into Ahmad and his friends Mahmood and Samirah.

toomaas:	ahlan yaa aHmad!	أهلاً يا أحمد!	توماس:
aHmad:	ahlan bik! kayf al-Haal?	أهلاً بك! كيف الحال؟	أحمد:
toomaas:	anaa bi-khayr. kayf Haalak?	أنا بخير. كيف حالك؟	توماس:
aHmad:	al-Hamdu lil-laah, kul shay' tamaam. haa'ulaa' aSdiqaa'ee. haathaa maHmood wa haathihi sameerah.	الحمد لله، كلّ شيء تمام. هؤلاء أصدقائي. هذا محمود وهذه سميرة.	أحمد:

toomaas:	tasharrafnaa. ahlan wa sahlan!	تَشَرَّفنا أهلاً أهلاً وسهلاً!	توماس:
maHmood:	ahlan bik! maa ismak?	أهلاً بك! ما اسمك؟	محمود:
toomaas:	ismee toomaas. min ayna antum?	اسمي توماس. من أين أنتم؟	توماس:
maHmood:	naHnu min al-urdunn wa sameerah filasTeeneeyah.	نحن من الأردنّ وسميرة فلسطينية.	محمود:
samirahh:	tatakallam 'arabee jayyidan!	تتكلّم عربي جيداً!	سميرة:
toomaas:	shukrann jazeelan.	شكراً جزيلاً.	توماس:
maHmood:	furSah sa'eedah yaa toomaas.	فرصة سعيدة يا توماس.	محمود:
toomaas:	furSah sa'eedah wa ma' as-salaamah!	فرصة سعيدة. ومع السلامة!	توماس:
aHmad:	ilaa al-liqaa' inshaa' allaah!	إلى اللقاء إن شاء الله!	أحمد:

المفردات

Vocabulary

The following vocabulary list for the dialogue you just read includes script, translation, and pronunciation. Try to write the words in order to get used to the Arabic script, then compare your writing with the original.

Name	ism	اِسْم
Nationality	jinseeyah	جِنْسِيّة
Egyptian (m)	miSree	مِصْري
date of birth	taareekh al-meelaad	تاريخ الميلاد
place of birth	makaan al-meelaad	مَكان الميلاد
Cairo	al-qaahirah	القاهِرة
Syrian (f)	sooreeyah	سوريّة
Damascus	dimashq	دِمَشْق
American (m)	amreekee	أمْريكي
American (f)	amreekeeyah	أمْريكيّة

Hi! (lit. Be a relative)	ahlan	أهلاً
(particle used in front of a name)	yaa	يا
(response to [ahlan]; lit. You be a relative)	ahlan bik	أهلاً بِكَ
how	kayfa	كَيْفَ
How are you? (lit. What's the condition?)	kayfa al-Haal	كَيْفَ الحالَ؟
I	anā	أنا
well/good (lit. with kindness)	bi-khayr	بِخَيْرٍ
How are you (m)? (lit. What's your condition?)	kayfa Haalak	كَيْفَ حالَكَ؟
Thank God (lit. God be praised)	al-Hamdu lil-laah	الحَمْدُ لله
everything	kull shay'	كُلّ شَيْء
good	tamaam	تمام
these are; these (pl with persons)	haa'ulaa'	هؤُلاء
my friends	aSdiqaa'ee	أصدِقائي
this is; this (m)	haathaa	هٰذا
and	wa	وَ
this is; this (f)	haathihi	هٰذه
my pleasure (lit. we are honored)	tasharrafnaa	تَشَرَّفْنا
Hi; A warm welcome (lit. be a relative and take it easy)	ahlan wa sahlan	أهلاً وسَهْلاً
What	maa	ما
What's your (m) name?	maa ismak	ما اسْمَكَ؟
My name is	ismee	اسْمي
What's your (f) name?	maa ismik	ما اسْمِك؟
from where	min ayna	مِنْ أَيْنَ
you (pl)	antum	أَنْتُمْ
we	naHnu	نَحْنُ
from	min	مِنْ
Jordan	al-urdunn	الأُرْدُنّ
Palestinian (f)	filasTeeneeyah	فِلَسْطينيَّة

(particle used in front of questions without question word)	hal	هَل
you (m, sing)	anta	أَنْتَ
No	laa	لا
you (inform) speak	tatakallam	تَتَكَلَّم
Arabic (m)	ʿarabee	عَرَبي
Yes	naʿam	نَعَم
I study/learn	adrus	أَدْرُس
In	fee	في
I like/love	uHibb	أُحِبّ
Language	lughah	لُغة
Well	jayyidan	جَيِّداً
thank you very much	shukran jazeelan	شُكراً جزيلاً
it was my pleasure (lit. happy opportunity)	furSah saʿeedah	فُرْصة سَعيدة
(good) bye (lit. with integrity)	maʿ as-salaamah	مَعَ السَّلامة
see you later (lit. until meeting)	ilaa al-liqaaʾ	إلَى اللِّقاء
God willing; hopefully	inshaaʾ allaah	إن شاء الله

Grammar القواعد

1. Personal Pronouns 4

Here is an overview of the personal pronouns that are used in spoken Arabic.

	singular			plural		
1st person	I	anaa	أنا	we	naHnu	نَحْنُ
2nd person	you (m)	anta	أَنْتَ	you	antum	أَنْتُم
	you (f)	anti	أَنْتِ			
3rd person	he	huwa	هُوَ	they	hum	هُم
	she	hiya	هِيَ			

In Arabic, there are no formal forms of address as there are in other languages. People address each other by their first name for example, Mr. Mahmood, Ms. Samirah or by their last name.
Only in very formal occasions will people use the 2nd person plural of *you* أَنْتُم [antum].

25

2. Simple Sentences with *to be* 6

Most simple sentences in Arabic are formed with *to be*.

I am from the USA.	anaa min amreekaa	أنا مِن أمْريكا.
Samirah is Palestinian.	sameerah filasTeeneeyah	سَميرة فلَسْطينيّة.
Where are you (pl) from?	min ayna antum	مِن أيْنَ أنْتُم؟

To ask the question form use هَل [hal], although in spoken Arabic this is generally dropped.

Are you (m) Jordanian?	hal anta 'urdunee	هَل أنْتَ أرْدُنّي؟
Are you (f) Jordanian?	hal anti urduneeyah	هَل أنْتِ أرْدُنّيّة؟

3. This Is, These Are 7

masculine		feminine		plural (with people)	
haathaa	هٰذا	haathihi	هٰذِه	haa'ulaa'	هٰؤُلاء

Examples:

This is Mahmood.	haathaa maHmood	هٰذا مَحْمود.
This is Samirah.	haathihi sameerah	هٰذِه سَميرة.
These are my friends.	haa'ulaa' aSdiqaa'ee	هٰؤُلاء أصْدِقائي.

When used in front of words with articles, they can sometimes take on the meaning *this/these*.

this name	haathaa al-ism	هٰذا الاسْم
these languages	haathihi al-lughaat	هٰذِه اللغات

To avoid confusion, you can add the appropriate personal pronoun.

This is (it) the name.	haathaa huwa al-ism	هٰذا هُوَ الاسْم

استعمال اللغة
Usage

Saying Hello and Good-bye 2

- Arabic greetings are sometimes very long and formal.
  When greeted with أَهْلاً [ahlan] or أَهْلاً وَسَهْلاً [ahlan wa-sahlan] respond with أَهْلاً بِك [ahlan bik].
- Asking about someone's well-being is part of a greeting and is often done several times. The response is always positive. When asked كَيْفَ الحَال؟ [kayfa al-Haal] you can answer with شُكْراً بِخَيْر [shukran bikhayr] or كُلّ شَيْء تَمام [kull shay' tamaam], and, if you want, you can thank God by saying الحَمْدُ لله [al-Hamdu lil-laah].
- When people are introduced to each other, تَشَرَّفْنا [tasharrafnaa] is appropriate.
  At the end of a conversation you can express your delight about meeting your new acquaintances by saying فُرْصة سَعيدة [furSah sa'eedah].
- When it's time to leave you can say مَع السَّلامة [ma' as-salaamah] or إلى اللِّقاء [ilaa al-liqaa'].
  إن شاء الله [inshaa' allaah] is always ideal, especially if you want to talk about the future or if you hope to meet this person again in the near future.

Culture Note

When greeting each other, a soft handshake is appropriate; followed by moving your hand to your heart. A man should wait to see if a woman wants to shake hands with him. If that's not the case, nod your head with a smile. Kisses on the cheeks and hugs are quite common between people of the same gender. In the Gulf states, some men greet each other by touching their noses.

More Useful Expressions
عبارات مفيدة أخرى

Below, you'll find additional useful words and phrases related to the topic of this lesson. Try to memorize them.

hello (lit. peace be with you)	as-salamu 'alaykum	السَّلام عَلَيْكُم
(response; lit. and with you peace)	wa-'alaykum as-salaam	وَعَلَيْكُم السَّلام
hi (lit. be welcomed)	marHaban	مَرْحَباً
(response; lit. you are welcome)	marHaban bik	مَرْحَباً بِك
good morning (lit. morning of goodness)	SabaaH al-khayr	صَباح الخَيْر
(response; lit. morning of light)	SabaaH an-noor	صَباح النُّور

27

good evening (lit. evening of goodness)	masaa' al-khayr	مَساء الخَيْر
(response; lit. evening of light)	masaa' an-noor	مَساء النُّور
good night (lit. happy night)	laylah sa'eedah	لَيْلة سَعيدة
(response)	laylah sa'eedah	لَيْلة سَعيدة
sleep well (awake in goodness)	tuSbiH 'alaa khayr	تُصْبِح عَلى خَيْر
(response; you too)	wa anta min ahlihe wa anta 'alaa khayr	وأَنْتَ مِن أَهْلِه وأَنْتَ عَلى خَيْر

 Regional Variations   في العامية

Language Note

Spoken Arabic differs from country to country. There are differences in pronunciation as well as vocabulary, and most dialects are not scripted. Because of the wide distribution of many Syrian and Egyptian films in the Arabic speaking world, both dialects are fairly well understood in Arabic speaking countries. On CD1 you'll also hear the dialogue in Syrian and Egyptian Arabic—Mahmood is from Egypt and Samirah is from Syria.

Regional Variations

	Syrian	Egyptian
answer to [ahlan wa sahlan]	ahlan fik	ahlan bik
How are you?	kifak	izzayak
Good.	mneeH	kwayyis
What's new? (lit. what are your news?)	shoo akhbaarak	akhbaarak ayh
These are my friends.	hadul rif'aatee	dul aSHaabee

	Syrian	Egyptian
That's Mahmood.	hay maHmood	dah maHmood
That's Samirah.	hay sameerah	di sameerah
What's your (m) name?	shoo ismak	ismak ayh
Where do you (pl) come from?	min wayn intu	intu min fayn
We	naHna	iHna
Yes	eh	aywa
this language	hal lughah	al-lughah di

Exercises
التمارين

1 Read Kareem's and Faatimah's ID cards again and mark the correct answers.

1. كريم عربي. ☐
2. كريم مصري. ☐
3. كريم من الأردنّ. ☐
4. فاطمة من سوريا. ☐
5. فاطمة من دمشق. ☐
6. فاطمة مصرية. ☐

2 What's the correct answer? Match the correct pairs as shown.

1. أهلاً وسهلاً!   a. فرصة سعيدة!
2. السلام عليكم!   b. وأنت على خير!
3. صباح الخير!   c. إلى اللقاء!
4. فرصة سعيدة!   d. أهلاً بك!
5. إلى اللقاء!   e. صباح النور!
6. تصبح على خير!   f. وعليكم السلام!

3 Complete the nationalities as shown in the example.

1. مصر   هو .. مصري ....   هي .. مصرية ....
2. سوريا   هو ....   هي ....
3. الأردنّ   هو ....   هي ....
4. فلسطين هو ....   هي ....

4 Fill in the personal pronouns.

1. اسْمي ناديا. .أنا .... فِلَسْطينيّة.
2. هٰؤلاء أصدقائي. .... من الأردنّ.
3. هٰذا كريم. .... مصري.
4. هٰذه فاطمة. .... سورية.
5. ما اسمك؟ .... و؟

5 Complete the form with your own information.

الاسم: .... تاريخ الميلاد: ....
الجنسية: .... مكان الميلاد: ....

6 Answer the questions.

1. كيف الحال؟ ...أنا بخير .... 3. من أين أنت؟ ....
2. ما اسمك؟ .... 4. أنت فِلَسْطينيّة ....

7 Imagine you're meeting Ahmad on the street. Greet him, ask him how he is, and introduce him to your friends Mahmood, Kareem, and Naadiyah.

1. أنت: ....! أهلاً يا أحمد!... → أحمد: أهلاً بكَ!
2. أنت: .... → أحمد: أنا بخير ، الحمد لله
3. أنت: .... أصدقائي.
4. .... محمود.
5. .... كريم.
6. و .... نادية. → أحمد: تشرّفنا.

In this lesson you will learn:
- **To book a hotel room**
- How to express *to have*
- **Personal suffixes**
- **Duality**
- **Roots and structures**

الدرس الثاني

مرحباً بكم في فندق الباشا!

Welcome to the Al-Baashaa Hotel!

فندقنا في قلب مدينة دهب.
كلّ غرفنا على البحر.
أَهْلاً وَسَهْلاً بكم وبأطفالكم
أيضاً في حديقتنا ومطعمنا!
إقامة سعيدة!

Our hotel is located in the heart of Dahab. All of our rooms have an ocean view. You and your children are also welcome in our garden and restaurant.

Have a pleasant stay!

What's New?

Personal Suffixes 4

ما الجديد؟

In this lesson you will learn about personal suffixes. They are usually added to a noun to show possession. Here is an overview.

	singular			plural		
1st person	my	-ee	ـِي	our	-naa	ـنَا
2nd person	your (m)	-ak	ـَك	your	-kum	ـكُم
	your (f)	-ik	ـِك			
3rd person	his	-uh	ـُه	their	-hum	ـهُم
	her	-haa	ـها			

By adding the personal suffix, the stress of pronunciation (in boldface) often moves to the next syllable.

hotel	funduq	فُنْدُق	→	our hotel	funduqnaa	فُنْدُقنا
rooms	ghuraf	غُرَف	→	our rooms	ghurafnaa	غُرَفنا
children	aTfaal	أَطْفال	→	your children	aTfaalkum	أَطْفالكُم
restaurant	maT'am	مَطْعَم	→	our restaurant	maT'amnaa	مَطْعَمنا

After attaching the personal suffix, the feminine ending taa' marbuta (ة) at the end of a word becomes taa' (ت).

| garden | Hadeeqah | حَديقة | → | our garden | Hadeeqatanaa | حَديقَتنا |

Personal suffixes can also be added to prepositions. مَرْحَباً بِك [marHaban bik] and أَهْلاً بِك [ahlan bik] always refers to only one person. When referring to several people use مَرْحَباً بِكُم [marHaban bikum] and أَهْلاً بِكُم [ahlan bikum]. السَّلامُ عَلَيْكُم [as-salaamu 'alaykum] also gets a suffix at the end.

bi-kam al-ghurfah?

بكم الغرفة؟

Thomas is at a hotel talking to the receptionist.

toomaas:	as-salaamu 'alaykum!	السلام عليكم!	:توماس
al-muwaTHaf:	wa 'alaykum as-salaam!	وعليكم السلام!	:الموظّف
toomaas:	'indkum ghurrfah bi-sareer waaHid?	عندكم غرفة بسرير واحد؟	:توماس
al-muwaTHaf:	laHTHah, min faDlak ... na'am, 'indanaa ghurfah.	لحظة ، من فضلك ... نعم ، عندنا غرفة.	:الموظّف
toomaas:	al-ghuraf bi-Hammaam wa ...? maa ismuh bi-l-'arabee? ... mukayyif?	الغرف بحمام و...؟ ما اسمه بالعربي؟ ... مكيّف؟	:توماس

al-muwaTHaf:	Tab'an!	طبعاً!	الموظّف:
toomaas:	bi-kam al-ghurfah?	بكم الغرفة؟	توماس:
al-muwaTHaf:	al-laylah bi-sab'at doolaaraat.	الليلة بسبعة دولارات.	الموظّف:
toomaas:	Tayyib. aakhuth haathihi al-ghurfah.	طيّب. آخذ هٰذه الغرفة.	توماس:
al-muwaTHaf:	kam laylah?	كم ليلة؟	الموظّف:
toomaas:	usboo'ayn.	أسبوعين.	توماس:
al-muwaTHaf:	a'Tinee jawaazak min faDlak.	أعطني جوازك من فضلك.	الموظّف:
toomaas:	'afwan? ... aah, fahimt. tafaDDal, haathaa jawaazee.	عفواً؟ ... آه ، فهمت. تفضّل ، هٰذا جوازي.	توماس:
al-muwaTHaf:	ahlan wa sahlan fee funduqnaa! tafaDDal, haathaa muftaaHak.	أهلاً وسهلاً في فندقنا! تفضّل ، هٰذا مفتاحك.	الموظّف:
toomaas:	shukran.	شكراً.	توماس:
al-muwaTHaf:	laa shukr 'alaa al-waajib.	لا شكر علىٰ الواجب.	الموظّف:

Vocabulary

المفردات

From now on in the wordlist you'll see both the singular form and plural form, separated by a diagonal slash. For the regular plural forms, only their ending is shown. Try to memorize the plural forms along with the singular forms.

hotel	funduq /fanaadiq	فُندُق / فَنادِق
heart	qalb	قَلْب
town	madeenah/mudun	مَدينَة / مُدُن
Dahab (ocean resort on Sinai)	dahab	دَهَب
every	kull	كُلّ
room	ghurfah/ghuraf	غُرْفَة / غُرَف
on	'alaa	علىٰ
sea	baHr	بَحْر
child	Tifl /aTfaal	طِفْل / أَطْفال
also	ayDan	أَيْضاً
garden	Hadeeqah/Hidaa'iq	حَديقة / جَدائِق

restaurant	maT'am/maTaa'im	مَطْعَم / مَطاعِم
Have a pleasant stay! (lit. a happy stay)	iqaamah sa'eedah	إقامة سَعيدة!
clerk; staff	muwaTHaf /--een	مُوَظَّف / ـين
at; with; to have	'ind	عِنْد
with; in	bi	بِـ
bed	sareer/asirrah	سَرير / أَسِرَّة
one	waaHid	واحِد
instant; moment	laHTHah/--aat	لَحْظة / ـات
please (m) (lit. from your (m) kindness)	min FaDlak	مِن فَضْلَك
please (f) (lit. from your (f) kindness)	min FaDlik	مِن فَضْلِك
bath (room)	Hammaam/--aat	حَمّام / ـات
What's that in Arabic? (lit. What is its name in Arabic?)	maa ismuh bi-l-'arabee	ما اِسمهُ بِالعَرَبي؟
air conditioning	mukayyif	مُكَيِّف
of course	Tab'an	طَبْعاً
how much (lit. for how much)	bi-kam	بِكَم
seven	sab'ah	سَبْعة
dollar	doolaar /--aat	دولار / ـات
good; OK	Tayyib	طَيِّب
I'll take	aakhuth	آخُذ
how many	kam	كَم
night	laylah/layaalee	لَيْلة / لَيالي
How many nights? (lit. How many night?)	kam laylah	كَم لَيْلة؟
Week	'usboo'/asaabee'	أُسْبوع / أسابيع
Give (m) me	a'Tinee	أَعْطِني
passport	jawaaz /--aat	جَواز / ـات
you're welcome!/Excuse me?	'afwan	عَفْواً
I understood	fahimt	فَهِمْت
Here (you go)	tafaDDal	تَفَضَّل
Mr.	sayyid / saadah	سَيِّد / سَادة
Key	miftaaH/mafaateeH	مِفتاح / مَفاتيح
No need for thanks. It's my duty.	laa shukr 'alaa l-waajib	لا شُكْر علىٰ الواجِب.

Grammar

القواعد

1. To Have 9

To express the English *to have*, you need to use the preposition عِنْد ['ind] *with* and add a personal suffix. Literally, you're saying *belonging to me/belonging to you/belonging to him…*

	singular			plural		
1st person	I have	['indee]	عِنْدي	we have	['indnaa]	عِنْدنا
2nd person	you (m) have	['indak]	عِنْدَك	you have	['indkum]	عِنْدكُم
	you (f) have	['indik]	عِنْدِك			
3rd person	he has	['induh]	عِنْدهُ	they have	['indhum]	عِنْدهُم
	she has	['indhaa]	عِنْدها			

2. Duality 9

Besides the singular and plural forms, Arabic also has a form to express the notion of the double as in *two weeks, two months* etc. The ending that you use for this double form is ـان [--aan] or ـيْن [--ayn]. In everyday speech, only the latter or the [ain] form is used. After attaching the double ending, the feminine ending taa' marbuta (ة) at the end of a word becomes [taa'] (ت).

| two weeks | 'usboo'ayn | أُسْبوعَيْن |
| two nights | laylatayn | لَيْلَتَيْن |

3. Regular Plural 8

Many plural forms that refer to people are regular. The masculine ending is ـون [--oon] or ـين [--een]. In everyday conversations, only the ending ـين [--een] is used. The feminine plural has the ending ـات [--aat] and, the taa' marbuta (ة) is dropped.

	masculine plural			feminine plural	
Egyptians	miSreeyeen	مِصْرِيّين		miSreeyaat	مِصْرِيّات
clerks	muwaTHafeen	مُوَظَّفين		muwaTHafaat	مُوَظَّفات

Words that don't end with a taa' marbuta (ة) can also have a feminine plural form, among them many words which are borrowed from other languages.

| passports | jawazaat | جَوازات |
| computers | kumbyootaraat | كُمْبيوتَرات |

In combination with personal suffixes the [noon] (ن) is dropped.

| your clerks | muwaTHafeekum | مُوَظَّفيكُم |

35

4. Irregular Plural

The plural form of the majority of Arabic words is irregular. Therefore, try to always memorize the singular and plural forms together.

The plural form of most of the nationalities is regular, but there are exceptions. The feminine forms, however, are always regular.

	masculine plural		feminine plural	
Arabs	ʻarab	عَرَب	ʻarabeeyaat	عَرَبيّات
English	inkleez	اِنْكليز	inkleezeeyaat	اِنْكليزيّات

5. Roots and Structures

Most Arabic words have a common root which consists of three or four consonants. For example, the root (ط — ب — خ) [t–b–kh] means *to cook*, and (ط — ع — م) [t-ʻ-m] means *to eat*. Short and long vowels between consonants, prefixes, and suffixes create structures which change the original meaning.

kitchen (location where meals are cooked)	maTbakh / maTaabikh	مَطْبَخ / مَطابِخ
restaurant (location where food is eaten)	maTʻam / maTaaʻim	مَطْعَم / مَطاعِم

To show the structures we'll use the root (ف — ع — ل) [f-ʻ-l] meaning *to do*, the consonants [f-ʻ-l] replacing other roots. مَفْعَل [mafʻal] for example is a structure for locations and is always in the plural form مَفاعِل [mafaaʻil]. Irregular plurals follow a variety of structures. The structure for the following plurals is أَفْعال [afʻaal].

Give examples:

children	aTfaal	أَطْفال
doors	abwaab	أَبْواب

Usage   استعمال اللغة

Important Polite Phrases

Here are a few phrases to use when asking for something, giving somebody something, or responding politely to someone.

- Use مِن فَضْلَك [min faDlak], if you want to ask someone for something or to ask a favor. When speaking to a woman say مِن فَضْلِك [min faDlik] and when speaking to more than one person say مِن فَضْلِكُم [min faDlikum].

| Just a moment, please. | laHTHah min faDlak | لَحْظة ، مِن فَضْلَك. |
| The key, please. | al-miftaaH min faDlak | المِفْتاح ، مِن فَضْلَك. |

- تَفَضَّل [tafaDDal] originates from the same root (ف – ض – ل) [f-D-l]. Use it when you give somebody something. The feminine form is تَفَضَّلي [tafaDDalee]. If you're talking to more than one person, use تَفَضَّلوا [tafaDDaloo].

| This is the key, here you are. | tafaddal hathaa al-miftaaH | تَفَضَّل ، هٰذا المِفْتاح. |

- The appropriate response to شُكْراً [shukran], is عَفْواً ['afwan] or لا شُكر على الواجب [laa shukr 'aala al-waajib]. عَفْواً ['afwan] intonated like a question changes its meaning to *Excuse me?* The same is true for نَعَم؟ [na'am?].

To Book a Hotel Room 3

Do you (pl) have a double room?	'indkum ghurfah bi-sareerayn	عِنْدكُم غُرْفة بِسَريرَيْن؟
How much is the room?	be-kam al-ghurfah	بِكَم الغُرْفة؟
Good, I'll take the room.	Tayyib, aakhuth al-ghurfah	طَيَّب ، آخُذ الغُرْفة.

More Useful Words: عبارات مفيدة أخرىٰ

Here are more words related to accommodations:

in/inside the house	fee al-bayt	في البَيْت
house, apartment	bayt/buyoot	بَيْت / بُيوت
door	baab /abwaab	باب / أبواب
kitchen	maTbakh/maTaabikh	مَطْبَخ / مَطابِخ
lamp	miSbaaH/maSaabeeH	مِصْباح / مَصابيح
chair	kursee/ karaasee	كُرْسي / كَراسي
wardrobe	khizaaanah/khazaa'in	خِزانَة / خَزائِن
bedroom	ghurfat an-nawm	غُرْفة النَّوْم

guest room	ghurfat aD-Duyoof	غُرْفة الضُّيُوف
living room	Saloon/--aat	صالون / ــات
table	Taawilah/--aat	طاولة / ــات
sofa	kanabah/--aat	كَنَبة / ــات
window	shubbaak/shabaabeek	شُبّاك / شَبابيك
carpet	sajaadah/sajajeed	سَجّادة / سَجاجيد

Regional Variations   في العامية

When you're listening to the Syrian and Egyptian dialogue you'll notice only slight differences when compared to the Modern Standard Arabic version. The only difference is often the pronunciation of some sounds or the fact that short vowels are either added or dropped.

The question word *what*?   11

The question word *what*, ما [maa], in Standard Arabic, is شو [shoo] in Syrian. In Egyptian, it is إيه [eh] and it is always placed at the end of the sentence. When asking for someone's name, use the question word *what*, the word اسم [ism] *name* and the personal suffix,-- as in *What is your/his/her name?*

MSA	Syrian 	Egyptian
What's your (m) name?	shoo ismak?	ismak eh?
What's your (f) name?	shoo ismik?	ismik eh?
What's his name?	shoo ismuh?	ismuh eh?
What's her name?	shoo ismah?	ismaha eh?

Exercises   التمارين

1   Read the hotel advertisement that appears on the first page of this lesson again and answer the questions using نَعَم [na'am] *yes* or لا [laa] *no*.

لا	نعم		
☐	☐	هل الفندق في القاهرة؟	1.
☐	☐	هل في الفندق حديقة؟	2.
☐	☐	هل في الفندق مطعم؟	3.

2 What would you say? Match each statement with the proper translation as shown in the example.

1. You'd like your room key.
2. You didn't understand.
3. You give the woman at the reception your passport.
4. She's thanking you, and you respond by saying: ...

a. عفواً.
b. مفتاحي ، من فضلك.
c. نعم؟
d. تفضّلي ، هذا جوازي.

3 You are at the reception of the Al-Baashaa hotel. Greet the receptionist and ask him if he has a single room. You want the room for two nights and you're asking how much it is.

1. أنت: .. مساء الخير! .... → الموظّف: مساء النور!
2. أنت: .... → الموظّف: كم ليلة؟
3. أنت: .... → الموظّف: نعم ، عندنا غرفة.
4. أنت: .... → الموظّف: الليلة بسبعة دولارات.

4 My town, your passport ... Complete the personal suffixes in the singular and plural.

	singular	جواز	plural	singular	مدينة	plural
1st person	....		....	.. مدينتي		....
2nd person	.. جوازك		....	....		....
3rd person	....		....	....		....
	....			....		

5 Write the dual or double form as shown in the example.

1. مدينة .. مدينتين ..
2. طفل ....
3. موظّف ....
4. غرفة ....
5. سرير ....
6. أسبوع ....

6 Which words share the same root? Match the pairs as shown in the example.

1. من فضلك
2. أسبوع
3. مصباح

a. صباح
b. سبعة
c. تفضّل

7 Complete the singular form.

1. مدن .... 3. ليالي .... 5. شَبابيك ....
2. جوازات .... 4. أسابيع .... 6. مفاتيح ....

8 Complete the plural form.

1. أردني .. أردّنيّين .... 3. طاولة .... 5. طفل ....
2. بيت .... 4. غرفة .... 6. سورية ....

9 Translate into Arabic.

1. *I have two children.* ....
2. *He has two passports.* ....
3. *We have a hotel.* ....
4. *Do you have a double room?* ....
5. *Do you have the key?* ....
6. *She has a garden.* ....

10 You are looking at various items and you're asking a friend from Syria what they are called in Arabic. Translate: "What do you call this in Arabic?"

....

11 Your Egyptian friend is showing you a photo of his daughter. Ask him: "What's her name?"

....

الدرس الثالث 3

In this lesson you will learn:
- Giving directions
- Adjectives
- Numbers up to 100
- Numbers with nouns
- Where places are located

City Map — خريطة المدينة

خريطة المدينة

National Museum	٤ المتحف الوطني	Old Market	١ السوق القديمة
Train station	٥ المحطّة	Big Mosque	٢ الجامع الكبير
New Square	٦ الساحة الجديدة	Palestine Street	٣ شارع فلسطين

What's New? / ما الجديد؟

Adjectives

Adjectives describe people, place and things. For example, the **old** town.
All adjectives have a masculine and feminine form. In most cases, the feminine adjective is created by adding the ending taa' marbuta (ة). Exceptions are marked with *(f)* in the glossary.

singular	masculine		feminine	
old	qadeem	قَديم	qadeemah	قَديمة
new	jadeed	جَديد	jadeedah	جَديدة
national	waTanee	وَطَني	waTaneeyah	وَطَنيّة

The plural of adjectives can also be regular or irregular. The taa' marbuta (ة) of the feminine plural becomes the ending ـات [--aat].

plural	masculine		feminine	
old	qudamaa'	قُدَماء	qadeemaat	قَديمات
new	judud	جُدُد	jadeedaat	جَديدات
national	waTaneeyeen'	وَطَنيّين	waTaneeyaat	وَطَنيّات

jaded fee al-madeenah / جديد في المدينة

Thomas is asking two people for directions to the National Museum.

toomaas:	'afwan yaa sayyidatee. ayna al-matHaf al-waTanee? hal huwa ba'aeed ?	توماس:	عفواً يا سيّدتي. أين المتحف الوطني؟ هل هو بعيد؟
as-sayyidah:	laa huwa qareeb! min hunaa ilaa shaari' filasTeen. wa ba'd thaalik 'alaa Tool ilaa as-saaHah al-jadeedah, wa min hunaak ilaa al-yasaar wa ba'd Hawaalee khamseen mitir binaayah qadeemah 'alaa al-yameen. al-matHaf janb haathihi al-binaayah.	السيّدة:	لا ، هو قريب! من هنا إلى شارع فلسطين. وبعد ذلك على طول إلى الساحة الجديدة ، ومن هناك إلى اليسار وبعد حوالي خمسين متر بناية قديمة على اليمين. المتحف جنب هذه البناية.
toomaas:	shukran jazeelan. ma' as-salaamah!	توماس:	شكراً جزيلاً. مع السلامة!

as-sayyidah:	allaah yisallmak!	السيّدة:	الله يسلّمك!

ba'd qaleel....

بعد قليل ...

toomaas:	law samaHat, hal ta'rif aT-Tareeq ilaa al-matHaf al-waTanee?	توماس:	لو سمحت ، هل تعرف الطريق إلى المتحف الوطني؟
as-sayyid:	maa'ah bil-maa'ah! ta'aal ma'ee!	السيّد:	مائة بالمائة! تعال معي!
toomaas:	alf shukr! anaa jadeed fee al-madeenah. anaa hunaa munthu thalaathat ayyaam.	توماس:	ألف شكر! أنا جديد في المدينة. أنا هنا منذ ثلاثة أيّام.
as-sayyid:	maa raayak bi-jawlah Sagheerah fee al-madeenah al-qadeemah.	السيّد:	ما رأيك بجولة صغيرة في المدينة القديمة؟
toomaas:	bi-kul suroor.	توماس:	بكلّ سرور!

المفردات

Vocabulary

The vocabulary in the word lists is always shown with vowel marks. To memorize the words in the correct vowel order, listen to the dialogues on the audio several times while reading along in the book.

map	khareeTah	خَريطة
market	sooq/aswaaq	سوق (f) / أَسْواق
old	qadeem/qudamaa'	قَديم / قُدَماء
mosque	jami'/jawaami'	جَامِع / جَوامِع
large; big	kabeer kibaar	كَبير / كِبار
street	shaari'/shawaari'	شارِع / شَوارِع
museum	matHaf/mataaHif	مَتْحَف / مَتاحِف
national	waTanee/--een	وَطَني / ـــين
train station; stop	maHaTTah/--aat	مَحَطّة / ـــات

square	saaHah/--aat	ساحة / سات
new	jadeed/judud	جَديد / جُدُد
woman; lady; ma'am	sayyidah/--aat	سَيِّدة / سات
where	'ayna	أَيْنَ
far	ba'eed	بَعيد
near; nearby	qareeb	قَريب
here	hunaa	هُنا
from here; this way	min hunaa	مِن هُنا
to	ilaa	إلى
after (time)	ba'd	بَعْد
after that	ba'd thaalik	بَعْد ذلِك
straight ahead	'aala Tool	عَلى طول
(over) there	hunaak	هُناك
the left	al-yasaar	اليَسار
about	Hawalee	حَوالي
fifty	khamseen	خَمْسين
meters	mitir/amtaar	مِتْر / أَمْتار
building	binaayah/--aat	بِناية / سات
on the right	'alaa al-yameen	عَلى اليَمين
next to	janb	جَنْب
(response to [ma'aa salama] ; lit. God is protecting you (m))	allaah yusallimak	ألله يُسَلِّمَك!
shortly afterwards (lit. after little)	ba'd qaleel	بَعْد قَليل
I'm sorry; allow (m) me	law samaHt	لَوْ سَمَحْت
you (m) know	ta'rif	تَعْرِف

way; road; route	Tareeq/Turuq	طَريق / طُرُق
one hundred percent (lit. hundred in hundred)	maaʾah bi-l-maaʾh	مائة بالمائة
Come! (m)	taʿaal	تَعال
with me	maʿee	مَعي
many thanks	alf shukr	أَلف شُكْر
since	munthu	مُنْذُ
three	thalaathaa	ثَلاثة
day	yawm/ayyaam	يَوْم / أَيّام
How about (lit. What's your(m) opinion about)	maa raʾyak (bi)	ما رَأيَك (بِـ)
tour	jawlah/--aat	جَوْلة / ـــات
little	Sagheer/Sighaar	صَغير / صِغار
with pleasure (lit. with every joy)	bi-kull suroor	بِكُلّ سُرور

Grammar القواعد

1. Adjectives 8,7,6

Unlike English, the adjectives in Arabic come after the noun. Both the nouns and adjectives in Arabic must agree in gender (masculine/feminine), state (definite/indefinite), case (genitive/nominative/accusative/sakoon), and number (singular/dual/plural).

a big street	shaariʿ kabeer	شارِع كَبير
a small building	binaayah Sagheerah	بِناية صَغيرة

The plural of an adjective is only used when the noun relates to people or persons. If the noun indicates objects, locations, etc., the singular feminine adjective form is used.

little children	aTfaal Sighaar	أَطْفال صِغار
old markets	aswaaq qadeemah	أَسْواق قَديمة

45

If the noun is defined by an article or personal suffix, the adjective needs an article.

the new station	al-maHaTTah al-jadeedah	المَحَطّة الجَديدة
our little children	aTfaalnaa aS-Sighaar	أطْفالنا الصِّغار

2. Adjectives With Simple *to Be* Sentences 9, 5

When adjectives are used in simple *to be* sentences, they do not have an article, but they have to agree with the gender of the noun. If the noun is plural and relates to people or persons, the plural form of the adjective is used. If it doesn't relate to people, the singular feminine adjective form is used.

The museum is near.	al-matHaf qareeb	المَتحَف قَريب.
The markets are old.	al-aswaaq qadeemah	الأسْواق قَديمة.
Our children are tall.	aTfaalnaa kibaar	أطْفالنا كِبار.

Nouns can be replaced with personal pronouns. Nouns that do not define people or persons are replaced by هي [hiya] and treated like feminine singulars.

It is near.	huwa qareeb	هُوَ قَريب.	←	The museum is near.	al-matHaf qareeb	المَتحَف قَريب.
It is old.	hiya qadeemah	هيَ قَديمة.	←	The market is old.	al-aswaaq qadeemah	الأسْواق قَديمة.
They are small/young.	hum Sighaar	هُم صِغار.	←	Our children are small/young.	atfaalna Sighaar	أطْفالنا صِغار.

3. Numbers up to 100 4

In the Pre-Lesson you already learned how to count to 10. The following numbers are composed as in English. *Fourteen* is أرْبَعَة عَشْر ['arba'at 'ashr], a combination of أرْبَعة ['arba'ah] and عَشَرة ['asharah]. The taa' marbuta (ة) of the first number is pronounced [at] and then connected with the shortened عَشْر ['ashr]. In the numbers *eleven* and *twelve*, the first digits are slightly different as is apparent below:

Numbers from 11 to 20						
11	iHdaa 'ashr	إحْدى عَشْر		16	sittat 'ashr	سِتّة عَشْر
12	ithnaa 'ashr	اثْنا عَشْر		17	sab'at 'ashr	سَبْعة عَشْر
13	thalaathat 'ashr	ثَلاثة عَشْر		18	thamaanyat 'ashr	ثَمانْية عَشْر
14	'arba'at 'ashr	أرْبَعة عَشْر		19	tis'at 'ashr	تِسْعة عَشْر
15	khamsat 'ashr	خَمْسة عَشْر		20	'ishreen	عِشْرين

After twenty, the order changes. First comes the ones, then the tens, with a وَ [wa] in between. Twenty one is therefore واحِد و عِشْرين [waaHid wa-'ishreen] (lit. one and twenty).

Numbers from 21 to 30

21	waaHid wa-'ishreen	واحِد وعِشرين	26	sittah wa-'ishreen	سِتّة وعِشرين
22	ithnayn wa-'ishreen	إثْنَيْن وعِشرين	27	sab'ah wa-'ishreen	سَبْعة وعِشرين
23	thalaathah wa-'ishreen	ثَلاثة وعِشرين	28	thamaanyah wa-'ishreen	ثَمانية وعِشرين
24	arba'ah wa-'ishreen	أرْبَعة وعِشرين	29	tis'ah wa-'ishreen	تِسْعة وعِشرين
25	khamsah wa-'ishreen	خَمْسة وعِشرين	30	thalaatheen	ثَلاثين

The tens are formed using the basic numeral without the taa' marbuta (ة) and the ending ـِين [-een].

Numbers from 40 to 110

40	'arba'een	أرْبَعين	80	thamaaneen	ثَمانين
50	khamseen	خَمْسين	90	tis'een	تِسْعين
60	sitteen	سِتّين	100	maa'ah	مائة
70	sab'een	سَبْعين	110	maa'ah wa-'asharah	مائة وعَشَرة

Between 100 and the number that follows insert, وَ [wa].

Note that مائة [maa'ah] can sometimes in Modern Standard Arabic be [mi'ah]. There's also a written variation, مِئة.

one hundred and sixty five	maa'ah wa khamsah wa sitteen	مائة وَخَمْسة وسِتّين

4. Numbers with Nouns   4

Combining nouns with numbers is not easy and sometimes even native speakers get confused. Here are the four most important rules:

▌ The number *one* is placed behind the noun like an adjective and always has the same gender as the noun.

one night	laylah waaHidah	لَيْلة واحِدة
one day	yawm waaHid	يَوْم واحِد

▌ If something is twice the number, the duality form must be used. The feminine ending taa' marbuta (ة) becomes taa' (ت). The word for *two* is not used.

two nights	laylatayn	لَيْلَتَيْن
two days	yawmayn	يَوْمَيْن

47

- In the numbers *three* to *ten*, the counted plural noun and the number word use the opposite gender. If the noun feminine, the number has to be masculine. If it's masculine, the number gets the feminine ending taa' marbuta (ة).

| three nights | thalaath layaalee | ثلاث لَيالي |
| three days | thalaathat ayaam | ثلاثة أَيّام |

- From *eleven* on, nouns are always in the singular.

| eleven nights | iHdaa 'ashr laylah | إحْدى عَشْر لَيْلة |
| twenty-three days | thalaathat wa-'ishreen yawm | ثلاثة وعِشْرين يَوْم |

Usage — استعمال اللغة

Asking for and Giving Directions 2, 1

This is how you ask for directions:

| Where is the train station? | ayna al-maHaTTah | أَيْنَ المَحَطّة؟ |
| Do you (m) know the way to the train station? | hal ta'rif aT-Tareeq ilaa al-maHaTTah? | هَل تَعْرِف الطَّريق إلى المَحَطّة؟ |

This is how to give directions:

from here/over there	min hunaa/hunaak	مِن هُنا / هُناك
straight ahead	'alaa Tool	على طول
to the right	ilaa al-yameen	إلى اليَمين
to the left	ilaa al-yasaar	إلى اليَسار
on the right (side)	'alaa al-yameen	على اليَمين
on the left (side)	'alaa al-yasaar	على اليَسار
after about 20 meters	ba'd Hawaalee 'ishreen mitir	بَعْد حَوالي عِشْرين مِتْر

More Useful Words

Where Places Are Located 10

عبارات مفيدة أخرى

to	ilaa	إلى
from	min	مِن
in	fee, bi	في ، بِـ
on; at	ʿalaa	عَلى
next to	janb	جَنب

across	muqaabil	مُقابِل
in front of	amaam	أَمام
behind	khalf	خَلْف
under	taHt	تَحْت
above	fawq	فَوْق

 **Regional Variations**

 في العامية

Where?

The question word *where*, in Standard Arabic is أَيْنَ [ayna], in Syrian is وين [wayn] and in Egyptian فين [fayn]. Therefore, *Where is the Nation Museum?* is:

in Syrian:	wayn il-matHaf/ MatHaf il-waTanee
in Egyptian:	fayn il-matHaf/ MatHaf il-waTanee

When listening to the Syrian and Egyptian variations of the dialogue on CD1, pay special attention to the answer given by the female speaker. Here are words that vary from Standard Arabic:

	Syrian	Egyptian
near; nearby	areeb	urayib
from here / to …	min hoon/la	min hina/liHad
from there to the left	baʿdeen	baʿad kidaa
there's an old building on	min huneek lashmaal	min hiaak shmaal
the right (side)	feeh binaayah adeemah ʿal-yameen	feeh mabna adeem ʿal-yameen
next to this building	iddaam hay al-binaayah	gamb il-mabna dih

Numbers

There are also variations in the pronunciation of numbers. Listen to the numbers from 1 to 20 first in Syrian, then in Egyptian on CD1.

Exercises / التمارين

1 You are standing in front of the National Museum. Ask for directions ...

a) to the old town ....

b) to the New Square ....

c) to the Big Mosque ....

2 Look at the map on the first page of this lesson. Where do the following directions take you?

من المتحف الوطني على طول إلى الساحة الجديدة. من هناك إلى اليسار. وبعد حوالي ثلاثين متر على اليمين.

Answer: ....

3 What are the opposites? Connect the appropriate words as shown.

a. قريب		1 هنا	
b. صغير		2 كبير	
c. قديم		3 بعيد	
d. هناك		4 أمام	
e. خلف		5 جديد	

4 Mark the correct singular or plural number form for the noun. The first one has already been done for you.

☒ أيّام	☐ يوم	٤	1.
☐ بنايات	☐ بناية	١٥	2.
☐ ليالي	☐ ليلة	٨٠	3.
☐ أمتار	☐ متر	٧	4.
☐ جوامع	☐ جامع	٩	5.
☐ طرق	☐ طريق	١٦٠	6.

5 Mark the correct translation.

1. الجامع الكبير
   - ☒ the big mosque
   - ☐ a big mosque

2. يوم جديد
   - ☐ the new day
   - ☐ a new day

3. الأسواق قديمة
   - ☐ the old markets
   - ☐ The markets are old.

4. بيتي قريب
   - ☐ my nearby house
   - ☐ My house is nearby.

6 Complete the adjectives as shown in the example.

1. غرفة (صغير) .. غرفة صغيرة .. 3. محطّة (كبير) ....
2. جواز (سوري) .... 4. مطعم (عربي) ....

7 Form the singular as shown in the example.

1. الشوارع الكبيرة .. الشارع الكبير .. 3. البنايات الجديدة ....
2. البيوت العربية .... 4. الأطفال الصغار ....

8 Form the plural as shown in the example.

1. مدينة جديدة .. مدن جديدة .. 3. الساحة القديمة ....
2. الحديقة الصغيرة .... 4. طاولة كبيرة ....

9 Replace the noun with the appropriate personal pronoun.

1. المتحف بعيد. .. هو بعيد .. 3. الأسواق قديمة. ....
2. المدينة كبيرة. .... 4. أصدقائي عرب. ....

10 The illustration below shows a hotel room. Fill in the correct prepositions from the box to describe the room.

| جنب | أمام | فوق | في ✓ | على |

1. في .. الغرفة سرير وطاولة وكرسي وخزانة.
2. السرير .... الخزانة.
3. الكرسي .... الطاولة.
4. .... الطاولة مصباح و .... الطاولة مفتاح.

51

In this lesson you will learn:
- Traffic signs
- Small talk
- Genitive constructions
- Negatives
- *To be* in the past tense
- Time indicators
- Locations

الدرس الرابع

إشارات المرور

Traffic Signs

to City Center	إلى مركز المدينة
to the Freeway	إلى الأتوستراد
to the Bus Station	إلى محطّة الباصات
to the Train Station	إلى محطّة القطار
to the Airport	إلى المطار

منطقة عسكرية
ممنوع التصوير

**Military Area
Photography Prohibited**

خفف السرعة

Reduce Speed

What's New? — ما الجديد؟

While in English compound constructions can also be in the genitive (e.g. *town center = center of town*), Arabic uses only the latter. The first noun always indicates the main word that is being described. If the main noun is feminine, the Ta' Marbuta (ة) [at] is pronounced.

the town center (lit. the center of the town)	markaz al-madeenah	مركز المدينة
the bus station (lit. the station of the bus)	maHaTTat al-baaSaat	محطّة الباصات

Adjectives or participles can also have such constructions.

Photography prohibited (lit. prohibiting of photographing)	mamnoo' at–taSweer	ممنوع التّصوير

ilaa markaz al-madeenah — إلى مركز المدينة

Thomas is standing on the sidewalk flagging down a taxi. The taxi stops and Thomas gets in.

toomaas:	SabaaH al-khayr!	صباح الخير!	توماس:
saa'iq at-taaksee:	SabaaH an-noor yaa sayyidee!	صباح النور يا سيّدي!	سائق التاكسي:
toomaas:	ilaa markaz al-madeenah, min faDlak.	إلى مركز المدينة، من فضلك.	توماس:
saa'iq at-taaksee:	'alaa 'aynee yaa sayyidee.	على عيني يا سيّدي.	سائق التاكسي:
toomaas:	wa hal 'andak 'addaad?	وهل عندك عدّاد؟	توماس:
saa'iq at-taaksee:	Tab'an, al-'addad hunaa … lughatak al-'arabeeyah mumtaazah!	طبعاً، العدّاد هنا … لغتك العربية ممتازة!	سائق التاكسي:
toomaas:	wa laakin al-'arabeeyah laysat sahlah.	ولكن العربية ليست سهلة.	توماس:
saa'iq at-taaksee:	hal kunt fee balad 'arabee min qabl?	هل كنت في بلد عربي من قبل؟	سائق التاكسي:
toomaas:	na'am, kunt fee al-maghrib qabl sanatayn wa fee al-imaaraat qabl thalaath sanawaat.	نعم، كنت في المغرب قبل سنتين وفي الإمارات قبل ثلاث سنوات.	توماس:
saa'iq at-taaksee:	wa maa ra'yak bi'aaSimat baladnaa al-jameel?	وما رأيك بعاصمة بلدنا الجميل؟	سائق التاكسي:
toomaas:	hiya jameelah jiddan wa an-naas Tayyibeen wa luTafaa'!	هي جميلة جدّاً والناس طيّبين ولطفاء!	توماس:
saa'iq at-taaksee:	tafaDDal yaa sayyidee, haathaa markaz al-madeenah.	تفضّل يا سيّدي، هذا مركز المدينة.	سائق التاكسي:
toomaas:	mumtaz, qif 'alaa al-yameen, min faDlak. kam al-ujrah?	ممتاز، قف على اليمين، فضلك. كم الأجرة؟	توماس:
saa'iq at-taaksee:	kamaa tureed.	كما تريد.	سائق التاكسي:

Vocabulary

المفردات

To get used to the non-vocalized script, from this lesson (lesson 4) on, the vowel mark Fatha will no longer appear in the text.
A short [a] in pronunciation will replace the vowel mark between two consonants.
All other marks mentioned in the Pre-Lesson remain.

sign	ishaarah	إشارة
traffic	muroor	مُرور
center	markaz/maraakiz	مركز / مراكِز
freeway	utoostraad	أُتوسْتْراد
bus	baaS/--aat	باص / ــات
train	qiTaar /--aat	قِطار / ــات
airport	maTaar/--at	مطار / ــات
Stop!	qif	قِف
Reduce! (lit. make easier)	khaffif	خفِّف
speed	sur'ah	سُرْعة
area	minTaqah	مِنْطقة
militarily	'askaree	عسْكري
prohibited	mamnoo'	ممْنوع
photographing	taSweer	تصْوير
driver	saa'iq/--een	سائِق / ــين
taxi	taaksee/takaasee	تاكْسي / تكاسي
certainly (lit. on my eye)	'alaa 'aynee	على عَيْني
you (m) (lit. your (m) presence)	haDritak	حضْرْتك
you (f) (lit. your (f) presence)	haDritik	حضْرْتِك
you (m) are not	lasta	لَسْتَ
you (f) are not	lasti	لَسْتِ
excuse me	law samaHt	لوْ سمحْت
car	sayyaarah/--aat	سيّارة / ــات
belt	Hizaam/'aHzimah	حِزام / أحْزِمة
safety	amaan	أمان
we are not	lasnaa	لسْنا

taxi meter	ʿadaad	عدّاد
of course	Tabʿan	طبْعاً
great, super	mumtaaz	مُمتاز
but	laakin	لكن
Arabic; the Arabic language	al-ʿarabeeyah	العربيّة
it (f) is not	laysat	لَيْست
simple, easy	sahl	سهْل
you (m) were; I was	kunt	كُنْت
country	balad/buldaan	بلد / بُلْدان
before; already	min qabl	مِن قبْل
Morocco	al-maghrib	المغْرِب
ago	qabl	قبْل
year	sanah/sanawaat	سنة / سنوات
United Arabic Emirates (UAE)	al-imaaraat	الإمارات
What's your opinion about	maa raʾyak (bi)	ما رأيك (ب)
capital	ʿaaSimah/ʿawaaSim	عاصِمة / عواصِم
beautiful, pretty, nice	jameel/--een	جميل / ــين
very	jiddan	جدّاً
people	naas	ناس
good; good-natured	Tayyib/--een	طيّب / ــين
friendly; nice	laTeef/luTafaaʾ	لطيف / لُطفاء
charge	ʾujrah	أجْرة
As much as you like. (lit. Suit yourself.)	kamaa tureed	كما تُريد

Grammar　　　　　　　　　　　　　　　　　　　　　　　القواعد

1. Genitive Constructions　3

The main word in a genitive construction never has an article. It is already defined when the accompanying noun has an article or personal suffix.

the taxi driver (lit. driver of the taxi)	saaʾiq at-taaksee	سائِق التّاكْسي
the capital of our country	ʿaaSimat baladnaa	عاصِمة بلدْنا

55

If the accompanying noun has no article, the genitive construction is indefinite.

| a taxi driver (lit. driver of a taxi) | saa'iq taaksee | سائِق تاكْسي |

The plural of a genitive construction is formed by putting the main word into the plural. Regular masculine plurals drop the ن (noon) of the plural ending ـين [-een].

| the taxi drivers | saa'iqee at-taaksee | سائِقي التّاكْسي |

2. Genitive Constructions with Adjectives 4

Adjectives always follow the genitive constructions whether they relate to the main noun or the word that accompanies it.

| the pretty capital of the country | 'aaSimat al-balad al-jameelah | عاصِمة البلد الجميلة |
| the capital of our pretty country | 'aaSimat baladnaa al-jameel | عاصِمة بلدنا الجميل |

If the accompanying noun is defined by an article or personal suffix, the adjective needs an article. If the genitive construction is indefinite, the adjective doesn't have an article.

| the friendly taxi driver | saa'iq at-taaksee al-laTeef | سائِق التّاكْسي اللّطيف |
| a friendly taxi driver | saa'iq at-taaksee laTeef | سائِق تاكْسي لطيف |

If the main noun and accompanying noun have the same gender, the adjective can relate to both nouns. The context defines how to translate such a phrase.

| the train station of the big city
or
the big train station of the city | maHaTTat al-madeenah –al-kabeerah | محطّة المدينة الكبيرة |

3. Negative Forms 6

The negative form is created by using *to be not* لَيْسَ [laysa]. The conjugated verb form appears either in the beginning of the sentence or after the subject. Personal pronouns can be recognized by the verb form and do not have to be written separately.

I'm not from here.	lastu min hunaa		لَسْتُ مِن هُنا.
It (f) is not easy.	laysat sahlah		لَيْسَت سهْلة.

The overview below shows how لَيْسَ [laysa] is conjugated. Keep in mind that Alif in the 3rd person plural form is not pronounced.

	singular				plural		
1st person	*I am not*	lastu	لَسْتُ		*we are not*	lasnaa	لَسْنا
2nd person	*you (m) are not*	lasta	لَسْتَ		*you are not*	lastum	لَسْتُم
	you (f) are not	lasti	لَسْتِ				
3rd person	*he is not*	laysa	لَيْسَ		*they are not*	laysoo	لَيْسوا
	she is not	laysat	لَيْسَت				

Plural forms that don't refer to people or persons are always treated as feminine singulars. The 3rd person plural form of the verb (لَيْسوا) is only used with people. The same is true for the demonstrative pronoun هؤُلاء [haa'ulaa'].

These houses are not old.	haathihi al-buyoot laysat qadeemah	هٰذِهِ البُيوت لَيْسَت قَديمة.
These people are not Egyptian.	haa'ulaa' an-naas laysoo miSreeyeen	هؤُلاء الناس لَيْسوا مِصرِيين.

4. Past Tense with *To be* in the past tense using كان [kaan]   9

To express the past you use the verb كان [kaan] *was/been*. Note that [kaan] is the informal form and [kaana] is the formal form. Its conjugation is similar to لَيْسَ [laysa]. The Alif of the ending in the 3rd person plural is not pronounced. Note that the verb forms of the 1st person singular and 2nd person singular *(m)* are identical. The context defines which person is meant.

	singular			plural		
1st person	I was	kunt	كُنْت	we were	kunnaa	كُنَّا
2nd person	you (m) were	kunt	كُنْت	you were	kuntum	كُنْتُم
	you (f) were	kunti	كُنْتِ			
3rd person	he was	kaan	كان	they were	kaanoo	كانوا
	she was	kaanat	كانَت			

Again, the personal pronouns here are already defined by the verb form. كان [kaan] as well as لَيْسَ [laysa] are positioned in the beginning of the sentence or after the subject. In questions, they are placed after the question word, just like in English. The 3rd person plural (كانوا) [kaanoo] is only used with people.

Where were you (pl)?	ayna kuntum	أَيْنَ كُنْتُم؟
We were in the center of town.	kunna fee markaz al-madeenah	كُنَّا في مرْكَز المدينة.
The markets were pretty.	al-aswaaq kaanat jameelah	الأسْواق كانت جميلة.
The people were nice.	an-naas kaanoo luTaafa' jiddan	النّاس كانوا لُطفاء جِدّاً.

Usage   استعمال اللغة

Time Indicators   8

Use these prepositions when talking about what happened when: مُنْذُ [munthu] *since, for*, قَبْل [qabl] *ago*; مِن قَبْل [min qabl] *before, already*. These time expressions are generally positioned at the end of the sentence.

| I've been in town for three days | anaa fee al-madeenah munthu thalaathat ayyaam | أنا في المدينة مُنْذُ ثلاثة أيّام. |

| I was in Egypt two years ago. | kunt fee miSr qabl sanatayn | كُنْت في مِصر قَبْل سنتَيْن. |
| We were here before. | kunnaa hunaa min qabl | كُنّا هُنا مِن قَبْل. |

More Useful Words عبارات مفيدة أخرىٰ

Roots and Structures — Locations 5,1

In Lesson 2 you've learnt about the structure مفاعل [mafaaʻil] for the irregular plural of location determiners. Many locations form their regular feminine plural forms with the ending ـات [--aat] as well.

in the city/town	fee al-madeenah	في المدينة
café	maqhaa /maqaahee	مقهىٰ / مقاهي
theater	masraH/masaariH	مسرح / مسارح
bank	maSraf/mSaarif	مصرف / مصارِف
harbor	meenaa'/mawaani'	ميناء / مَوانِئ
school	madrasah/madaaris	مدرسة / مدارس
library; book store	maktabah/--aat	مكتبة / ـات
university	jaamiʻah/--aat	جامعة / ـات
movie theater	seenimaa/seenimaat	سينما / سينمات
hospital	mustashfaa/mustashfayaat	مُسْتَشْفىٰ

Culture Note

Taxis in Arabic cities are cheap and preferable to public busses. Most taxis have meters. During rush hour, at night, or for unusual routes, it is advisable to negotiate the fare in advance. The invitation to pay as much as you'd like is just a polite phrase. It is better to offer a fair price and then negotiate if necessary.

Regional Variations

في العامية

Negative Forms ت10

Modern Standard Arabic (MSA) لَيْسَ [laysa] is not used in dialects. The negative forms of simple sentences are in Syrian مو [moo] and مُش [mush] in Egyptian.

	Syrian	Egyptian
You (m) are not from here.	Hadritak moo min hoon	Hadritak mush min hinaa
We are not in Germany.	naHnaa moo bi-al-maanyaa	iHnaa mush fee almaanyaa
Arabic is not easy.	il-'arabee moo sahil	il-'arabee mush sahl

Exercises — التمارين

1 Sort the words from the boxes either under "in the house" or "in town".

| مطبخ | باص | طاولة | سيّارة | شارع | باب | غرفة | ساحة |

في البيت	في المدينة
....	....
....	....

2 Match the genitive constructions with their English translations as shown in the example.

a. the bank clerk
b. the house door
c. the children's room
d. the bus
e. the school building
f. the kitchen cabinet

1 باب البيت
2 محطّة الباصات
3 غرفة الأطفال
4 موظّف المصرف
5 خزانة المطبخ
6 بناية المدرسة

3 Form meaningful genitive constructions using the words in the boxes.

أطفال	باص	جامعة	سيّارة	مكتبة	سائق	مفتاح	باب
....		....		....		....	
....		....		....		....	
....		....		....		....	

4 Translate into Arabic.

1. the little bedroom   .. غرفة النوم الصغيرة ....

2. the old town center   ....

3. a big school building   ....

4. nice taxi drivers   ....

5 Which of the words in the boxes form their plural with the structure مفاعل and which ones are in the regular feminine plural? Enter them in the chart as shown in the example.

متحف	محطّة	مطعم	سينما	مكتبة	مدرسة	مطار	مركز

plural after structure مفاعل		regular feminine plural	
....	.. مراكز	....	.. مطارات
....	....	....	....

6 Put these sentences into the negative using the correct form of ليس, as shown in the example.

1. أنا إنكليزي. .. لست إنكليزي. ....
2. نحن من ألمانيا. ....
3. الجامعة قريبة. ....
4. السوق كبيرة. ....

7 Put these sentences into the past tense using the correct form of كان as shown in the example.

1 المدينة كبيرة. .. المدينة كانت كبيرة. ....

2 العاصمة جميلة. ....

3 نحن في بلد عربي. ....

4 الناس طيّبين ولطفاء. ....

8 Put the prepositions قبل , منذ or من قبل in their appropriate place.

1 أنا في المغرب .... يومين.   3. كنّا في مصر .... خمس سنوات.

2 كنتم في العاصمة .... ؟   4. كنت في دمشق .... أسبوع.

9 Read the dialogue from this lesson again and answer the questions in complete sentences.

1 هل كان توماس في بلد عربي من قبل؟ ....

2 أين كان؟ ....

10 Write the negative forms of these sentences in Syrian and Egyptian.

    Syrian   Egyptian

1 المدرسة بعيدة.   a. ....   b. ....

2 هو من مصر.   a. ....   b. ....

62

Test 1

1 Read Samirah's travel diary and decide which statements are true (T) or false (F).

الأربعاء: ذهبنا إلىٰ المتحف المصري. هو قريب من فندقنا.
الخميس: كنّا عند الأهرام. هي كبيرة جدّاً.
الجمعة: شربنا قهوة في مقهىٰ صغير وكتبت رسائل إلىٰ الأصدقاء.
السبت: اليوم ذهبنا إلىٰ السوق واشترينا أشياء كثيرة.

		T	F
1.	It's far from the hotel to the Egyptian Museum.	☐	☐
2.	Samirah and Mahmood were at the Pyramids on Wednesday.	☐	☐
3.	Restaurants and coffee shops are closed on Fridays.	☐	☐
4.	Samirah bought a lot of things at the souk (market).	☐	☐

Points ...../4

2 Write the opposites.

1. هناك   ....   3. قريب   ....   5. بعد   ....
2. جديد   ....   4. فوق   ....   6. صغير   ....

Points ...../6

3 Which word doesn't fit into each category? Mark it.

1.	باص ☐	سيّارة ☐	سيّد ☐	قطار ☐
2.	مطبخ ☐	بلد ☐	حمّام ☐	صالون ☐
3.	طاولة ☐	كرسي ☐	خزانة ☐	صديق ☐
4.	مفتاح ☐	ساحة ☐	مدينة ☐	شارع ☐
5.	يوم ☐	أسبوع ☐	قهوة ☐	سنة ☐
6.	جواز ☐	موظّف ☐	طفل ☐	سائق ☐

Points ...../6

4 Write the plurals of these locations.

1. متحف   ....   3. مطبخ   ....   5. مكتب   ....
2. مطعم   ....   4. مركز   ....   6. مدرسة   ....

Points ...../6

63

5 Which adjective form fits the appropriate noun?

1. فندق	☐ قديم	☐ قديمة	☐ قدماء	☐ قديمات	
2. سيّارات	☐ جديد	☐ جديدة	☐ جدد	☐ جديدات	
3. أطفال	☐ صغير	☐ صغيرة	☐ صغار	☐ صغيرات	
4. أشياء	☐ كثير	☐ كثيرة	☐ كثيرين	☐ كثيرات	
5. موظّفة	☐ لطيف	☐ لطيفة	☐ لطفاء	☐ لطيفات	
6. سيّدات	☐ جميل	☐ جميلة	☐ جميلين	☐ جميلات	

Points ...../6

6 Match the correct answer to each question.

1. ما اسمك؟	a.	كنت في السينما.	
2. من أين أنتم؟	b.	في الساعة تسعة ونصف.	
3. أين المصرف؟	c.	بخمسة عشر دولار.	
4. ماذا فعلت أمس؟	d.	نحن من الإمارات.	
5. بكم الغرفة بسريرين؟	e.	اسمي كريم.	
6. في أيّ ساعة الموعد؟	f.	هو مقابل الجامعة.	

Points ...../6

Total ...../34

In this lesson you will learn:
- To talk about past events
- To tell time
- Days of the week
- The Question word ماذا
- Accusative

الدرس الخامس
5

رسالة من القاهرة

A Letter from Cairo

My dear Faatimah,

Hello,

How are you? I hope you are doing well. We're in Cairo for five days and I have fallen in love with this city from the minute I got here. We did alot. We were at the Pyramids and at the Egyptian Museum. We have been drinking coffee and tea at the coffee shops and we have been to the market where we bought a beautiful carpet.

See you soon,

Your friend Samirah
and your friend Mahmood

عزيزتي فاطمة
تحيّة طيّبة وبعد ...
كيف حالك؟ إن شاء الله بخير.
نحن في القاهرة منذ خمسة أيّام وأحبّ هذه المدينة منذ الدقيقة الأولى. فعلنا أشياء كثيرة: كنّا عند الأهرام وفي المتحف المصري. شربنا قهوة وشاي في المقاهي وذهبنا إلى السوق. هناك اشترينا سجّادة شرقية جميلة.
إلى اللقاء القريب!

صديقتك سميرة
وصديقك محمود

What's New?

Roots and Structures — Verbs in the Past Tense   1

In Arabic there is only one past tense form, ذهْبنا [thahabnaa]. It can mean *we went* or *we have gone*. Personal pronouns are already part of the conjugated verb form.

| We went to the market. We've gone to the market. | thahabnaa ilaa as-sooq | ذهبْنا إلى السّوق. |

In order to express the infinitive, use the 3rd person singular (*m*) of the past tense. Therefore, ذهب [thahab] means *he went* or *he is gone*, and stands for the infinitive *to go* as well.

The verbs are generally conjugated using the verb فعل [faʻal] *to do*. The consonants (ف – ع – ل) [f-ʻ-l] function as place holders for other root consonants.

Note that the verb forms of the 1st person singular and the 2nd person singular (*m*) are identical. The context helps you determine the person.

	singular				plural		
1st person	I have made	faʻalt	فَعَلْــتُ		we have made	faʻalnaa	فَعَلْــنا
2nd person	you (m) have made	faʻalt	فَعَلْــتَ		you have made	faʻaltum	فَعَلْــتُم
	you (f) have made	faʻalti	فَعَلْــتِ				
3rd person	he has made	faʻal	فَعَل		they have made	faʻaloo	فَعَلــوا
	she has made	faʻalat	فَعَلَــتْ				

If the consonants (ذ – ه – ب) [th-h-b] are inserted, you'll get the conjugation of the verb ذهب [thahab] *to go*. The endings are the same for all verbs.

	singular				plural		
1st person	I went	thahabt	ذَهَبْــتُ		we went	thahabnaa	ذَهَبْــنا
2nd person	you (m) went	thahabt	ذَهَبْــتَ		you went	thahabtum	ذَهَبْــتُم
	you (f) went	thahabti	ذَهَبْــتِ				
3rd person	he went	thahab	ذَهَب		they went	thahaboo	ذَهَبــوا
	she went	thahabat	ذَهَبَــتْ				

○ على التليفون

○ 'alaa at-taleefoon

Samirah talks to her friend Fatima.

samirah:	aaloo!	آلو!	سميرة:
faaTimah:	marHaban yaa samirah! kayfa Haalik?	مرحباً يا سميرة! كيف حالك؟	فاطمة:
samirah:	al-Hamdu lil-laah, anaa bikhayr. man ma'ee?	الحمد لله، أنا بخير. من معي؟	سميرة:
faaTimah:	anaa faaTimah.	أنا فاطمة.	فاطمة:
samirah:	ahlann yaa faaTimah! Kayfa al-Haal?	أهلاً يا فاطمة! كيف الحال؟	سميرة:
faaTimah:	kul shay' tamaam. ittaSalt biki ams. ayna kunti? maathaa fa'alti?	كلّ شيء تمام. اتّصلت بك أمس. أين كنت؟ ماذا فعلت؟	فاطمة:
samirah:	fee aS-SabaaH kunt fee al-maktab wa katabt rasaa'il. ba'da aTH-THuhur ishtareet ashyaa' min as-sooq. wa fee al-masaa' thahabt ma' aSdiqaa'ee ilaa as-seenimaa.	في الصباح كنت في المكتب وكتبت رسائل. بعد الظهر اشتريت أشياء من السوق. وفي المساء ذهبت مع أصدقائي إلىٰ السينما.	سميرة:
faaTimah:	'indik waqt al-yawm?	عندك وقت اليوم؟	فاطمة:
samirah:	kam as-saa'ah al-aan?	كم الساعة الآن؟	سميرة:
faaTimah:	as-saa'ah waaHidah.	الساعة واحدة.	فاطمة:
samirah:	anaa aasifah, 'indee maw'id fee as-saa'ah ithnayn wa niSf. laakin 'indee waqt ghadan.	أنا آسفة، عندي موعد في الساعة اثنين ونصف. لكن عندي وقت غداً.	سميرة:
faaTimah:	'aTHeem! ta'aalee 'indnaa fee al-masaa'!	عظيم! تعالي عندنا في المساء!	فاطمة:
samirah:	bikul suroor! fee ayy saa'ah?	بكلّ سرور! في أيّ ساعة؟	سميرة:
faaTimah:	fee as-saa'ah thamaaneeyah.	في الساعة ثمانية.	فاطمة:
samirah:	mumtaaz. ilaa yawm al-ghad, in shaa' allaah!	ممتاز. إلىٰ يوم الغد، إن شاء الله!	سميرة:

Vocabulary   المفردات

letter	risaalah/rasaa'il	رِسالة / رَسائِل
My dear (f) (address in private letters)	ʿazeezatee	عزيزتي
Greetings to you. (phrase to begin a letter)	taHeeyah Tayyibah wa-baʿad	تَحيّة طيِّبة وبَعْد ...
I love	ʾuHibb	أُحِبّ
minute	daqeeqah/daqaaʾiq	دَقيقة / دَقائِق
the first minute	ad-daqeeqah al-ʾoolaa	الدَّقيقة الأُولَىٰ
to do; to make	faʿal	فَعَل
thing; something	shayʾ/ashyaaʾ	شَيْء / أشْياء
much	katheer/--een	كَثير / ــين
pyramid	haram/ahraam	هرم / أهْرام
to drink	sharib	شَرِب
coffee	qahwah	قَهْوة
tea	shaay	شاي
to go, to walk	thahab	ذَهب
to buy	ʾishtaraa	اِشْتَرىٰ
oriental; middle eastern	sharqee/--een	شَرْقي / ــين
friend	Sadeeq/aSdiqaaʾ	صَديق / أصْدِقاء
telephone	tileefoon	تِليفون
hello! (on the phone)	aaloo	آلو
Who's there? (lit. Who's with me?)	man maʿee	مَن معي؟
to telephone, to call	ʾitaSal (bi)	اِتَّصل (بِـ)
I called you (f)	ʾitaSalt biki	اِتَّصلْت بِكِ
yesterday	ams	أمْس
what (in questions with verbs)	maathaa	ماذا
in the morning	fi asS-SabaaH	في الصَّباح
office	maktab/makaatib	مكْتَب / مكاتِب
to write	katab	كتب
in the afternoon	bʿad aTH-THuhr	بَعْد الظُّهْر
in the evening	fee al-masaaʾ	في المَساء
time	waqt/awqaat	وقْت / أوْقات
today	al-yawm	اليَوْم
hour; clock	saaʿah /--aat	ساعة / ــات
What time is it? (lit. How much is the hour?)	kam as-saaʿah	كَم السَّاعة؟
now	al-aan	الآن
I'm sorry.	anaa aasif (ah)	أنا آسِف (ــة).

appointment	maw'id / mawaa'eed	مَوْعِد / مَواعيد
half	niSf	نِصْف
tomorrow	ghadan	غَداً
excellent	'aTHeem	عظيم
come!	ta'aalaa	تَعالى
with pleasure	bi-kull suroor	بِكُلّ سُرور
which	ayy	أيّ
At what time? (lit. to which hour?)	fee ayy saa'ah	في أيّ ساعة؟
tomorrow (lit. the day tomorrow)	yawm al-ghad	يَوْم الغَد

Grammar القواعد

1. Roots and Structures — the Verbs شرب and اشترى   1, 2

In some verbs, the vowel after the second root consonant is *i*, e.g in شرب [sharib] *to drink*. Other verbs have so-called weak root consonants that turn into a diphthong [see pg 16] or vowel, or they disappear altogether, e.g. اشترى [ishtaraa] *to buy*. The last root consonant here is [yaa'] (ي).

to drink		شَرِب
I drank	sharibt	شَرِبْت
you (m) drank	sharibt	شَرِبْت
she (m) drank	sharibat	شَرِبَت
they drank	shariboo	شَرِبوا

to buy		اِشْتَرى
I bought	ishtarayt	اِشْتَرَيْت
you (m) bought	ishtarayt	اِشْتَرَيْت
she (m) bought	ishtarat	اِشْتَرَت
they bought	ishtaraoo	اِشْتَرَوْا

2. The Question Word ماذا   2

You are already familiar with the question word ما [maa] *what* for questions without verbs. If the question contains a verb, use the question word ماذا [maathaa].

What is that?	maa haathaa	ما هٰذا؟
What did you do?	maathaa fa'altum	ماذا فعلْتُم؟

3. The Accusative   3

In spoken Modern Standard Arabic (MSA), e.g. in broadcasts, speeches, or talks, nouns and adjectives share the same endings for the nominative, genitive, and accusative cases. The words are linked together and the pronunciation has a more melodic sound. The words themselves do not change. The only ending which is written in the non-vocalized script is the accusative ending ـاً [-an]. This ending appears with masculine indefinite words which are placed after verbs as direct complements. The accusative case marks the direct object in a sentence. The direct object is the object that receives the direction. There are various endings used to mark the accusative case; depending on the number, gender and definiteness of the noun or adjective in question. Definite singular masculine and feminine nouns and adjectives are marked by fatha which is written as (َ), and sounds like a short /a/.

Indefinite singular masculine nouns and adjectives are marked by a double fatha which is written as (ً) and has the sound /an/.

Note that the double fatha, when written over indefinite feminine nouns ending in taa' marbuta appears only as (ةً / ـةً) without the associated alif.

| We bought a lamp. | ishtaraynaa miSbaaHan | اِشْتَرَيْنا مِصْباحاً. |

In everyday speech these endings are not pronounced. To account for this fact, you will not see these accusative endings in the dialogues or spoken parts, e.g. often in adverbs:

| in the mornings | SabaaHan | صَباحاً | in the evenings | masaa'an | مَساءً |
| at noon | THuhran | ظُهْراً | at night | laylan | لَيْلاً |

4. Telling Time 4, 3

In Modern Standard Arabic (on television, in time announcements, etc.) the time of day is always expressed with ordinal numbers. In everyday speech, cardinal numbers are used.

| What time is it? (lit. How much is the hour?) | kam as-saa'ah | كم السّاعة؟ |
| It's six o'clock. | as-saa'ah sittah | السّاعة سِتّة. |

The time of the day is expressed by using the numbers *one* to *twelve*. If you want to be more specific, simply add time determiners.

6:00 in the morning	as-saa'ah sittah SabaaHan	السّاعة سِتّة صَباحاً
1:00 in the afternoon	as-saa'ah waaHidah THuhran	السّاعة واحِدة ظُهْراً
3:00 in the afternoon	as-saa'ah thalaathah ba'd aTH-THuhr	السّاعة ثلاثة بَعْد الظُهْر
6:00 in the evening	as-saa'ah sittah masaa'an	السّاعة سِتّة مَساءً
1:00 at night	as-saa'ah waaHidah laylan	السّاعة واحِدة لَيْلاً

Time segments after each hour are expressed by adding و [wa] *and*. There's رُبْع [rub'] *a quarter* as well as نِصْف [niSf] *half*. In addition, there is ثُلْث [thulth] *a third*. The rules for minutes follow the rules in Lesson 3, connecting numbers with nouns.

6:10	as-saa'ah sittah wa-'ashr daqaa'iq	السّاعة سِتّة وعَشر دقائق
6:15	as-saa'ah sittah wa-rub'	السّاعة سِتّة ورُبْع
6:20	as-saa'ah sittah wa-thulth	السّاعة سِتّة وثُلْث
6:25	as-saa'ah sittah wa-khams wa-'ishreen daqeeqah	السّاعة سِتّة وخَمْس وعِشْرين دقيقة
6:30	as-saa'ah sittah wa-niSf	السّاعة سِتّة ونِصْف

When approaching the top of the hour, the preposition إلاّ [illaa] *except* is used. Literally, 6:45 would be *7:00 except a quarter*.

6:45	as-saaʻah sabʻah illaa rubʻ	السّاعة سَبْعة إلاّ رُبْع
6:55	as-saaʻah sabʻah illaa khams daqaaʼiq	السّاعة سَبْعة إلاّ خَمْس دقائِق

Usage   استعمال اللغة

Time Indicators 5

now	al-aan	الآن	in the morning	fee aS-SabaaH	في الصّباح
yesterday	ams	أمس	at noon	fee aTH-THuhr	في الظُّهْر
today	al-yawm	اليَوْم	in the afternoon	baʻd aTH-THuhr	بعد الظُّهْر
tomorrow	ghadan	غداً	in the evening	fee al-masaaʼ	في المساء

To Make an Appointment 5

Do you (m/f) have time?	ʻindak/indik waqt	عِنْدَك وقْت؟
Yes, I have time.	naʻam, ʻindee waqt	نعم ، عِنْدي وقْت.
I'm sorry, I have an appointment.	anaa aasif(--ah), ʻindee mawʻid	أنا آسِف (ــة). عِنْدي مَوْعِد.
At what time?	fee ayy saaʻah	في أيّ ساعة؟
At 8:00.	fee as-saaʻah thamaaneeyah	في السّاعة ثَمانية.

Useful Words   عبارات مفيدة أخرى

The Days of the Week أيام الأسبوع 5

The days of the week are either expressed as in the table below or with the added term يَوْم [yawm] *day*, e.g. الأحد [al-aHad] or يَوْم الأحد [yawm al-aHad] *Sunday*.

Sunday	al-aHad	الأحد	Thursday	al-khamees	الخميس
Monday	al-ithnayn	الإثْنَين	Friday	al-jumʻah	الجُمْعة
Tuesday	ath-thulaathaaʼ	الثّلاثاء	Saturday	as-sabt	السَّبْت
Wednesday	al-ʼarbiʻaaʼ	الأرْبِعاء			

Culture Note

Friday يَوْم الجُمْعة [yawm al-jumʻah] is the Islamic holy day of the week where observing Muslims meet at the mosque الجامع [al-jaamiʻ] to hear their sermon (root: ج — م — ع, [j-m-ʻ] *to gather, to come together*.) In some countries, official institutions are closed on Thursdays and Saturdays as well. Christian businesses and schools are closed on Sundays.

Regional Variations

في العامية

The Verb [raaH] راح 6

Syrian Arabic and Egyptian Arabic sometimes use words that only exist in their dialects. Instead of ذهب [dahab] the verb راح [raaH] is used. Note that the ending of the 2nd person plural is shortened when spoken in dialect.

	singular			plural		
1st person	I went	ruHt	رُحْت	we went	ruHnaa	رُحْنا
2nd person	you (m) went	ruHt	رُحْت	you went	ruHtoo	رُحْتوا
	you (f) went	ruHti	رُحْتِ			
3rd person	he went	raaH	راح	they went	raaHoo	راحوا
	she went	raaHit	راحِت			

Regional Vocabulary 8, 7

	Syrian	Egyptian
yesterday	imbaariH	imbaariH
What did you do?	shu saawayt(--i)?	'amalt(--i)/eh?
letter	risaalah/rasaa'il	gawaab/--aat
(various) things	shaghlaat	Hagaat
time	wa't	wa't
today	il-yawm	in-nahaar dah
What time is it?	addesh is-saa'ah	is-saa'ah kaam
now	halla'	dilwa'ti
tomorrow	bukrah	bukrah

التمارين

Exercises

1 Read the letter on the first page of this lesson again. What would Samirah have written had she traveled by herself? Use the verb forms from the boxes to complete the sentences as shown in the example.

ذهبت	شربت	كنت	فعلت	اشتريت

1. ..فعلت........... أشياء كثيرة.
2. .... عند الأهرام وفي المتحف المصري.
3. .... قهوة وشاي في المقاهي.
4. .... إلى السوق.
5. .... سجّادة شرقية جميلة.

2 Samirah is calling her friend Faatimah to tell her what she did yesterday. Listen to the dialogue again and answer the questions.

1. ماذا فعلَت في الصباح؟ .. كانت في المكتب وكتبت رسائل. ....
2. ماذا فعلَت بعد الظهر؟ ....
3. ماذا فعلَت في المساء؟ ....

3 Fill in the time of the day as shown in the example.

ليلاً	ظهراً	صباحاً	مساءً	بعد الظهر	
			الساعة اثنا عشر	noon	1.
		..ظهراً..			
			الساعة اثنين ونصف	2:30 pm	2.
			الساعة تسعة وربع	9:15 pm	3.
			الساعة واحدة وثلث	1:20 am	4.
			الساعة سبعة إلاّ ربع	6:45 am	5.

4 كم الساعة؟ What time is it? Write the times as shown in the example.

1. 11:00   الساعة احدىٰ عشر..
2. 3:10   ....
3. 5:20   ....
4. 6:30   ....
5. 9:45   ....

5 Do you have free time or do you have an appointment? To answer the questions, use two variations as shown in the example.

عندك وقت الآن؟   1. نعم ، عندي وقت.   2. أنا آسف (ـة) ،عندي موعد.

عندك وقت اليوم؟   3. ....   4. ....

عندك وقت الخميس؟   5. ....   6. ....

6 Where did they go? Change the sentences from the 3rd person singular (m) into the 3rd person plural as shown in the example.

1. راح إلىٰ السينما. .. راحوا إلىٰ السينما.   ....
2. راح إلىٰ السوق.   ....
3. راح إلىٰ الجامعة.   ....

7 Translate the following sentence from the Syrian dialect into Modern Standard Arabic and into Egyptian Arabic.

Syrian: [shu saawayt imbaariH?]   Standard Arabic: 1. ....
                                   Egyptian: 2. ....

8 Translate this short dialogue into Modern Standard Arabic.

Egyptian: ● ['andak wa'it in-nahaar dah?]   Modern Standard Arabic: 1. ....
          ● [bukrah, in shaa allaah.]   2. ....

الدرس السادس

In this lesson you will learn:
- Information about your family
- Professions
- Talking about age
- Present tense
- Future tense
- Adverbs

An Egyptian Film

فيلم مصري

You Are My Life

Director:	Khaled Youssef
Actors:	Hani Salama (Yussif)
	Menna Shalabi (Yussif's wife)
	Hashem Selim (doctor)
	Nelly Kareem (Schams)

Yussif is an engineer, he is married, and has a son. The small family lives in the town of Hurghada. But there is a problem: Yussif is ill. He goes to the doctor where he meets the dancer Schams and he falls in love with her. Then his wife finds out and the problems begin.

أنت عمري

المخرج: خالد يوسف
الممثّلين: هاني سلامة (يوسف)
منّة شلبي (زوجة يوسف)
هاشم سليم (الطبيب)
نيللي كريم (شمس)

يوسف مهندس ، متزوّج وعنده ابن. تسكن العائلة الصغيرة في مدينة الغردقة. لكن هناك مشكلة ، يوسف مريض. يذهب إلى الطبيب ويقابل هناك الراقصة شمس ويقع في الحبّ. ثمّ تعرف زوجته القصّة وتبدأ المشاكل.

What's New?   ما الجديد؟

Roots and Structures — Verbs in the Present Tense   5

Like the past tense, in the present tense the personal pronoun is already part of the conjugated verb form.

| He goes to the doctor. | yathhab ilaa al-Tabeeb | يذْهَبُ إلى الطبيب. |

Present tense conjugations are characterized by prefixes and endings. In the example verb فعل [faʻal] *to make* the consonants ف – ع – ل [f-ʻ-l] function as place holders.
Note that the verb forms of the 2nd person singular (*m*) and the 3rd person singular (*f*) are identical. The context determines which person is meant.

	singular			plural		
1st person	I make	afʻal	أَفْعَل	we make	nafʻal	نَفْعَل
2nd person	you (m) make	tafʻal	تَفْعَل	you make	tafʻaloon	تَفْعَلون
	you (f) make	tafʻaleen	تَفْعَلين			
3rd person	he makes	yafʻal	يَفْعَل	they make	yafʻaloon	يَفْعَلون
	she makes	tafʻal	تَفْعَل			

The verb ذهب *to go* follows the same pattern.

	singular			plural		
1st person	I go	athhab	أَذْهَب	we go	nathhab	نَذْهَب
2nd person	you (m) go	tathhab	تَذْهَب	you go	tathhaboon	تَذْهَبون
	you (f) go	tathhabeen	تَذْهَبين			
3rd person	he goes	yathhab	يَذْهَب	they go	yathhaboon	يَذْهَبون
	she goes	tathhab	تَذْهَب			

في مقهى أبو سعيد / fee maqhaa aboo sa'eed

Ahmad and Thomas go to a coffee shop and sit down at one of the tables.

aHmad wa toomaas yathhaboon ilaa al-maqhaa wa yajlisoon

أحمد وتوماس يذهبون إلىٰ المقهىٰ ويجلسون ...

aHmad:	haathaa maqhaa aboo sa'eed. aboo sa'eed laTeef jiddan. sawfa taraa.	أحمد: هٰذا مقهىٰ أبو سعيد. أبو سعيد لطيف جدّاً. سوف ترىٰ.
aboo sa'eed:	masaa' alkhayr yaa shabaab!	أبو سعيد: مساء الخير يا شباب!
aHmad:	masaa' an-noor yaa aboo sa'eed! kayf al-aHwaal? kayf al-'aailah?	أحمد: مساء النور يا أبو سعيد! كيف الأحوال؟ كيف العائلة؟
aboo sa'eed:	wal-laahi, kul shay' tamaam. maathaa tashraboon?	أبو سعيد: والله، كلّ شيء تمام. ماذا تشربون؟
aHmad:	shaay, min faDlak.	أحمد: شاي، من فضلك.
aboo sa'eed:	fawran! ... man haathaa?	أبو سعيد: فوراً! ...من هذا؟
aHmad:	haathaa Sadeeqee toomaas. yadrus al-lughah al-'arabeeyah wa sayashtaghil hunaa fee al-mustashfaa.	أحمد: هٰذا صديقي توماس يدرس اللغة العربية وسيشتغل هنا في المستشفىٰ.
aboo sa'eed:	marHaban bik! anaa aboo sa'eed. tafham 'arabee?	أبو سعيد: مرحباً بك! أنا أبو سعيد. تفهم عربي؟
toomaas:	atakallam 'arabee qaleelan.	توماس: أتكلّم عربي قليلاً.
aboo sa'eed:	anta mutazawwij?	أبو سعيد: أنت متزوّج؟
toomaas:	na'am, zawjatee tashtaghil kamuhandisah fee sharikah 'aalameeyah.	توماس: نعم، زوجتي تشتغل كمهندسة في شركة عالمية.
aboo sa'eed:	wa maathaa tashtaghil anta?	أبو سعيد: وماذا تشتغل أنت؟
toomaas:	anaa Tabeeb.	توماس: أنا طبيب.
aboo sa'eed:	'andak aTfaal?	أبو سعيد: عندك أطفال؟
toomaas:	na'am, 'indee walad wa bint.	توماس: نعم، عندي ولد وبنت.
aboo sa'eed:	kam 'umruh?	أبو سعيد: كم عمرهم؟
toomaas:	ibnee 'umruh sitt sanawaat. wa bintee, 'umrhaa arba' sanawaat.	توماس: ابني، عمره ستّ سنوات. وبنتي، عمرها أربع سنوات.
aboo sa'eed:	maa shaa' allaah.	أبو سعيد: ما شاء الله!

77

Vocabulary
المفردات

film	feelm/aflaam	فيلم / أفلام
life; age	'umr	عُمر
film director (m)	mukhrij/--een	مُخْرِج / ــين
actor (m)	muththil/--een	مُمَثِّل / ــين
wife	zawjah	زَوْجة
doctor (m)	Tabeeb/aTibbaa'	طبيب / أطِبّاء
engineer (m)	muhandis/--een	مُهَنْدِس / ــين
married	mutazawwij/--een	مُتَزَوِّج / ــين
son	ibn/abnaa'	اِبْن / أبْناء
to live; to reside	sakan -- yaskun	سكن – يَسْكُن
extended family	'aailah/--aat	عائِلة / ــات
Hurghada (resort town)	al-ghardaqah	الغَرْدَقة
problem	mushkilah/ mashaakil	مُشْكِلة / مَشاكِل
sick	mareeD	مَريض
to go	thahab -- yathhab	ذهب – يَذْهَب
to meet	qaabal -- yuqaabil	قابل – يُقابِل
dancer (f)	raaqiSah	راقِصة
to fall	waqa' -- yaqa'	وقع – يقع
love	Hubb	حُبّ
to fall in love	waqa' fee al-Hubb	وقع في الحُبّ
then	thumm	ثُمّ
to know; to find out	'arif – ya'rif	عرف – يَعْرِف
story	qiSSah	قِصّة
to begin; to start	bada' – yabda'	بدأ – يَبْدأ
to sit	jalas -- yajlis	جلس – يَجْلِس
future tense participle	sawfa	سَوْفَ

to see	ra'aa -- yaraa	رأى – يَرَى
young man, (pl:) youth	shaab/shabaab	شاب / شباب
Guys! (inf)	yaa shabaab	يا شباب!
condition	Haal/aHwaal	حال / أحْوال
How are you?	kayf al-aHwaal	كَيْف الأحْوال؟
How's the family?	kayf al-'aailah	كَيْف العائِلة؟
God (is my witness)!	wa allaah	والله!
to drink	sharib -- yashrab	شرب – يَشْرب
right away; at once	fawran	فَوْراً
who	man	مَن
Who is this?	man haathaa	مَن هٰذا؟
to learn, to study	dars -- yadrus	درس – يَدرُس
future tense prefix	sa	سَـ
to work	ishtaghal -- yashtaghil	اِشْتغل – يَشْتَغِل
to understand	fahim -- yafham	فهم – يفْهم
to speak	takallam -- yatakallam	تكلّم – يَتكلّم
less (adv)	qaliilan	قَليلاً
as	ka	كَـ
engineer (f)	muhandisah/--aat	مُهَنْدِسة / ــات
company	sharikah/--aat	شَرِكة / ــات
international	'aalamee/--een	عالَمي / ــين
boy; son, (pl:) children	wald/awlaad	ولد / أولاد
girl; daughter	bint/banaat	بِنْت (f) / بنات
How old are they?	kam 'umruhum	كم عُمْرُهُم؟
What is God's will! (expression of admiration)	maa shaa' allaah!	ما شاء الله!

القواعد
rammar

1. Roots and Structures — Middle Vowel

In the present tense, verbs have the middle vowels **a**, **u**, or **i**. There are no rules here. Try to memorize each one when learning the verb forms of the 3rd person singular (m) in the past and in the present tense. Example: ذهب — يذْهب [thahab -- yathhab], درس — يدْرُس [dars - yadrus] and عرف — يعْرِف [ʿarif - yaʿrif].

to study		درس — يـدْرُس	to know		عرف — يـعْرِف
I study	adrus	أدْرُس	I know	aʿrif	أعْرِف
you (m) study	tadrus	تـدْرُس	you (m) know	taʿrif	تـعْرِف
she studies	tardus	تـدْرُس	she knows	taʿrif	تـعْرِف
they study	yadrusoon	يـدْرُسـون	they know	yaʿrifoon	يـعْرِفـون

2. Word Order in Regular Sentences

The subject of a sentence can be positioned in front of the verb or behind it. The sequence in everyday conversations is often subject–verb. In written Arabic, the verb–subject order is much more common.

subject–verb:	zawjee yashtaghil ka-muhandis	My husband works as an engineer.	زَوْجي يشْتغِل كَمُهنْدِس.
verb–subject:	taskun al-ʿaailah fee al-ghardaqah	The family lives in Hurghada.	تسكُن العائلة في الغرْدقة.

In the beginning of a sentence, the verb has to be in the singular, even if the subject is plural. If the subject doesn't relate to people, the 3rd person singular (f) verb form is used.

The friends go to the coffee shop.	yathhab al-aSdiqaaʾ ilaa al-maqhaa	يذْهب الأصْدِقاء إلى المقْهى.
I had problems. (lit. With me were problems.)	kaanat ʿindee mashaakil	كانَت عنْدي مشاكِل.

3. Roots and Structures — The Verb رأى (saw)

The verb رأى — يرَى [raʾaa – yaraa] to see has a yaaʾ (ي) as the last root consonant which can turn into a diphthong [au, ai] or a vowel at the conjugation. In addition, the hamza (ء) is dropped when conjugating the present tense forms.

past tense			present tense		
I saw; you (m) saw	raʾayt	رَأَيْت	I see	araa	أرَى
she saw	raʾat	رَأَت	you (m) see / she sees	taraa	تـرَى
they saw	raʾaw	رَأَوْا	they see	yarawn	يـرَوْن

4. The Future Tense   6

The future tense is expressed by using the present tense verb form and adding the particle سَوْفَ [sawfa] or its short form سَـ [sa-] as a prefix.

| You (m) will see. | sawfa taraa | سَوْفَ تَرَىٰ. |
| He will work in the hospital. | sayashtaghil fee al-mustashfaa | سَيَشْتَغِل في المُسْتَشْفىٰ. |

5. Roots and Structures — Adverbs

Adjectives become adverbs when they relate to a verb. Adverbs have the accusative ending [an] ـً .

| We have seen much. | ra'aynaa katheeran | كثير | → | رَأينا كثيراً. |
| I speak (a) little Arabic. | atakallam 'arabiiyah qaleelan | قليل | → | تكلّم عربية قليلاً. |

Culture Note   استعمال اللغة

Common Arabic Expressions With the Word الله (God).

To speak the word *God* is considered highly commendable. أُذْكُر الله [uthkur allaah] *Mention God* is a motto in إسلام [islaam] *Islam*. Therefore you will find many expressions that contain the word الله [allaah] *God*. They are very common in everyday speech, often as an expression of emotion or phrase.

God is most great!	allahu akbar	الله كبر!
In the name of God! (before you start doing something)	bismi-llaah	بِسْم الله!
The praise belongs to God! (along with good news)	al-Hamdu lillaah	الحَمْدُ لله!
Oh my God! (to reaffirm: Honestly!; horrified: Oh God!)	wa allaah	والله!
God willing! (when talking about the future: Hopefully!)	in shaa' allaah	إن شاء الله!
What God wants! (expressing admiration: How nice!)	maa shaa' allaah	ما شاء الله!

Usage

Talking About Job And Family 7, 2

Are you (m/f) married?	anta/ti mutazawwij/ah	أَنْتَ مُتَزَوِّج (ـة)؟
I'm married.	anaa mutazawwij/ah	أنا مُتَزَوِّج (ـة).
I'm single.	anaa 'aazib/ah	أنا عازِب (ـة).
She is divorced.	hiya muTallaqah	هي مُطلّقة.
He is widowed.	huwa armal	هُو أَرْمل.
What's your (m) profession?	maathaa tashtaghil?	ماذا تشْتغِل؟
What's your (f) profession?	maathaa tashtaghileen?	ماذا تشْتغِلين؟

Do you have children?	'indak/ik aTfaal?	عِنْدَك أطْفال؟
I have no children.	maa 'indee aTfall	ما عِنْدي أطْفال.
I have a son.	'indee ibn	عِنْدي اِبْن.
I have a daughter.	'indhaa bint	عِنْدها بْنت.
He has two sons.	'indhu ibnayn	عِنْدهُ ابْنَيْن.
I'm an engineer.	anaa muhandis/ah	أنا مُهنْدس (ـة).
I work at a company.	ishtaghil fee sharikah	أشْتغِل في شرِكة.

عُمْر means *life* as well as *age*. To say how old someone or something is, say literally *my, your, his age is ...* .

How old are you (m/f)	kam 'umrak/ik	كم عُمْرَك؟
I'm 30 years old.	'umree thalaatheen sanah	عُمْري ثلاثين سنة.

How old is she?	kam 'umrhaa?	كم عُمْرها؟
She's 8 years old.	'umrhaa thamaanee sanawaat	عُمْرها ثماني سنوات.

Useful Words عبارات مفيدة أخرى

Roots and Structures — Professions 4, 3

The following professions are written with their masculine form. For the feminine form, add taa' marbuta (ة). The plural ending is ـات [--aat].

Professions with Nisba-ending		
journalist	SaHafee/--een	صحفي / ـين
police man	shurTee/--een	شُرْطي / ـين
pharmacist	Saydalee/Sayaadilah	صَيْدلي / صيادلة
mechanic	meekaaneekee/--een	ميكانيكي / ـين

Professions with فاعِل [faa'il] structure		
scientist	'aalim/'ulamaa'	عالِم / عُلماء
student	Taalib/Tullaab	طالِب / طُلّاب
merchant	taajir/tujjaar	تاجِر / تُجّار
worker	'aamil/'ummaal	عامِل / عُمّال

81

Professions with [fa''aal] فَعَّال structure

hair stylist	Hallaaq/--een	حلّاق / ـين
baker	khabbaaz/--een	خبّاز / ـين
chef	Tabbaakh/--een	طبّاخ / ـين
artist	fannaan/--een	فنّان / ـين

Professions with prefix [mu] مُ

teacher	mudarris/--een	مُدرِّس / ـين
photographer	muSawwir/--een	مُصوِّر / ـين
translator/interpreter	mutarjim/--een	مُتَرْجِم / ـين
executive	mudeer/-een	مُدير / ـين

Culture Note

The family is the center of everyday life. Asking about one's family is part of all greetings. When meeting someone, exchanging information about one's family is more important than the person's job or career. If you are not married and you have no children, there's really only one response: قريباً ، إن شاء الله! [qareeban, in shaa' allaah] *Hopefully soon!*

  Regional Variations

The Verb شاف

When speaking in dialect, instead of [ra'aa] رأى use the verb [shaaf] شاف. In present tense conjugations, you often see a baa' (ب) in front of the verb.

past tense			present tense		
I saw; you (m) saw	shuft	شُفْت	I see	bshoof	بْشوف
she saw	shaafit	شافِت	you (m) see / she sees	bitshoof	بِتْشوف
they saw	shaafoo	شافوا	they see	beeshoofoo	بيشوفوا

Future Tense in Non-Standard Arabic

In non-Standard Arabic, instead of the particle [sawfa] سَوْفَ use the particle [haa] ها in front of the present tense verb form. The baa' (ب) in front of the verb is dropped.

| You (m) will see. | haat-shoof | ها تْشوف. |
| He will work in the hospital. | haa yishtaghil fee al-mustashfaa | ها بِشْتغل في المُسْتشْفىٰ. |

Regional Vocabulary

	Syrian	Egyptian
coffee shop	ma'haa	ahwaa
very	kteer	giddan
Who is that?	meen haad/hai?	meen dah/di?
This is my friend.	haathaa rafee'ee	dah saaHbee
I speak a little Arabic.	baHki 'arabee shwayya	batkallim 'arabee shwayya
Are you (m) married?	inta mitzawwij?	inta mitgawwiz?
my wife	martee	maraatee
doctor, physician	duktoor	duktoor
How old are they?	addaysh 'umruhum	'umruhum addeh

التمارين

Exercises

1 Read the information about the film on the first page of this lesson again. Then decide which of the statements are true (T) or false (F).

	T	F	
1	☒	☐	يوسف مهندس.
2	☐	☐	عند يوسف بنت.
3	☐	☐	تسكن العائلة في القاهرة.
4	☐	☐	زوجة يوسف طبيبة.
5	☐	☐	اسم الراقصة شمس.

2 Listen to the dialogue again and answer the questions.

1 إلى أين ذهب أحمد وتوماس؟ .. ذهبوا إلى المقهى ....
2 ماذا شربوا؟ ....
3 هل توماس متزوّج؟ ....
4 ماذا تشتغل زوجة توماس؟ ....
5 كم عمر ابن توماس؟ ....
6 كم عمر بنته؟ ....

3 Who works where? Fill in the blanks as shown in the example.

الطبّاخ	الطبيب	السائق	المدرّس	الراقصة	التاجر

1 من يشتغل في المستشفى؟	.. يشتغل الطبيب في المستشفى ....
2 من يشتغل في السوق؟	....
3 من تشتغل في المسرح؟	....
4 من يشتغل في المدرسة؟	....
5 من يشتغل في السيّارة؟	....
6 من يشتغل في المطبخ؟	....

4 Write the feminine forms of these professions as shown in the example.

1 موظّف	..موظّفة...........	4. مهندس	....
2 مترجم	....	5. طالب	....
3 صيدلي	....	6. حلّاق	....

84

5 Transform these sentences from the past tense into the present tense form.

1. ذهب إلى الجامعة. .. يذهب إلى الجامعة. ....
2. شربوا قهوة. ....
3. عرفتِ كثيراً. ....
4. رأيت الأهرام في مصر. ....
5. سكنَت العائلة في دمشق. ....
6. درسنا اللغة العربية. ....

6 Write the future tense forms using the prefix ـس as shown in the example.

1. يتكلّمون اللغة الألمانية. .. سيتكلّمون اللغة الألمانية. ....
2. يشتغل في شركة. ....
3. تفهم العربية. ....
4. أين نجلس؟ ....
5. ماذا يفعل؟ ....
6. تسكنون في الفندق. ....

7 Answer these questions in your own words.

1. كم عمرك؟ ....
2. أنت متزوّج (ـة)؟ ....
3. عندك أطفال؟ ....
4. ماذا تشتغل (ـين)؟ ....

الدرس السابع ٧

In this lesson you will learn:
- **Apologizing**
- **Shopping and negotiating**
- **Numbers to 1000**
- **Colors**
- **Verbs with prepositions**
- **Personal suffixes with prepositions**
- **More Prepositions**
- **Imperative form**

محل للشرقيات

هل تحتاجون إلى هدية أو تبحثون عن تحف شرقية؟
نقدّم لكم مصنوعات يدوية من الذهب والفضّة والنحاس ، بالإضافة إلى ذلك مصنوعات الموزاييك وأقمشة شرقية بأشكال وألوان كثيرة. ستشترون عندنا فقط منتجات بجودة عالية وأسعار رخيصة.
تجدون محلّنا في سوق الحميدية في دمشق القديمة. إسألوا عن محلّ « الشام للشرقيات ».

A Store Specializing in Middle Eastern Products

Are you looking for a present or rarities from the Middle East?

We carry hand-made products made of gold, silver, and brass, also mosaic items and Middle Eastern fabrics in many shapes and colors. Purchase high quality products at bargain prices. You'll find our store in the al-Hameediya souk in the old part of Damascus. Ask for the store called "**[ash-shaam li-sh-sharqeeyaat]**".

What's New? / ما الجديد؟

Verbs with Prepositions 2

The verb [iHtaaj -- yaHtaaj] اِحْتاج – يَحْتاج *to need* can only have an object if it is connected with the preposition [ilaa] إلى. Some verbs require a specific preposition which has to be memorized together with the verb.

Examples: [baHath – yabHath ('an)] بحث – يبحث (عن) *to look (for)* and [sa'al – yas'al ('an)] سأل – يسأل (عن) *to ask (for)*.

I need a present.	aHtaaj ilaa hadeeyah	أحْتاج إلى هديّة.
I'm looking for a store.	abHath 'an maHall	أبحث عن محلّ.
I asked for the prices. (or: you (m) asked)	sa'alt 'an al-as'aar	سألت عن الأسعار.

fee as-sooq / في السوق

Ahmad is looking for a present and talks to a vendor at the souk.

at-taajir:	marHaban yaa ustaath! tafaDDal!	مرحباً يا أستاذ! تفضّل! — التاجر:
aHmad:	marHaban bik, aHtaaj ilaa hadeeyah wa abHath 'an shay' sharqee.	مرحباً بك ، أحتاج إلى هدية وأبحث عن شيء شرقي. — أحمد:
at-taajir:	ahlan wa sahlan! 'indee kull shay'. narjeelaat wa thahab wa fiDDah wa aqmishah…	أهلاً وسهلاً! عندي كلّ شيء. نرجيلات وذهب وفضّة وأقمشة… — التاجر:
aHmad:	mumkin araa an-narjeelaat?	ممكن أرى النرجيلات؟ — أحمد:
at-taajir:	Tab'an, 'indee alwaan wa ashkaal katheerah. tashrab shaay?	طبعاً. عندي ألوان وأشكال كثيرة. تشرب شاي؟ — التاجر:
aHmad:	na'am ma' sukkar qaleel, law samaHt.	نعم ، مع سكّر قليل ، لو سمحت. — أحمد:
at-taajir:	tafaDDal, ijlis hunaa yaa ustaath!	تفضّل ، إجلس هنا يا أستاذ! — التاجر:

87

aHmad:	law samaHt, bikam haathihi an-narjeelah aS-Safraa' al-kabeerah?	لو سمحت ، بكم هٰذه النرجيلة الصفراء الكبيرة؟	أحمد:
at-taajir:	hiya rakheeSah jiddan ! bitis'amaa'at layrah faqaT.	هي رخيصة جداً. بتسعمائة ليرة فقط.	التاجر:
aHmad:	haathaa ghaalee jiddan! adfa' faqaT sitmaa'at layrah.	هٰذا غالي جدّاً! أدفع فقط ستّمائة ليرة.	أحمد:
at-taajir:	wal-laah, mustaHeel! haathihi an-narjeelah bijoodah 'aaleeyah! khuth waaHidah Sagheerah! haathihi an-narjeelah al-Hamraa' rakheeSah, bethamaan-maa'at layrah faqaT.	والله ، مستحيل! هٰذه النرجيلة بجودة عالية! خذ واحدة صغيرة! هٰذه النرجيلة الحمراء رخيصة ، بثمانمائة ليرة فقط.	التاجر:
aHmad:	wa az-zarqaa' hunaak, bikam haathihi?	والزرقاء هناك ، بكم هٰذه؟	أحمد:
at-taajir:	a'mal lak sa'r jayyid. sab'a-maa'ah wa khamseen layrah.	أعمل لك سعر جيّد. سبعمائة وخمسين ليرة.	التاجر:
aHmad:	indee faqaT sab sab'a-maa'at layrah.	عندي فقط سبعمائة ليرة.	أحمد:
at-taajir:	wal-laah, anta Sa'b. Tayyib, an-narjeelah bi sab sab'a-maa'at layrah.	والله ، أنت صعب. طيب ، النرجيلة بسبعمائة ليرة.	التاجر:
aHmad:	Tayyib, aakhuth an-narjeelah az-zarqaa'.	طيّب ، آخذ النرجيلة الزرقاء.	أحمد:
at-taajir:	mabrook yaa ustaath. hiya filan hadeeyah jameelah.	مبروك يا أستاذ. هي فعلاً هدية جميلة.	التاجر:
aHmad:	allah yubaarik feek.	الله يبارك فيك.	أحمد:

Vocabulary

المفردات

to need	iHtaaj -- yaHtaaj (ilaa)	اِحْتاج – يِحْتاج (إلى)	handmade	yadawee	ـدوي
present, gift	hadeeyah/hadaayaa	هديّة / هدايا	gold	thahab	ـهب
or	aw	أوْ	silver	fiDDah	ـضّة
to look (for)	baHath – yabHath ('an)	بحَث – يِبْحث (عن)	brass	nuHaas	ـاس
rarity	tuHfah/tuHaf	تُحْفة / تُحَف	in addition	bil-iDaafah ilaa thaalik	الإضافة إلى ذلك
to present	qaddam – yuqaddim (li)	قدّم – يُقدِّم (لِ)	mosaic	muzaayeek	ـوزاييك
we present you	nuqaddam lakum	نُقدِّم لَكُم	fabric	qumaash/aqmishah	ـاش / أقمِشة
			form, shape	shakl/ashkaal	ـكْل / أشْكال
product	maSnoo'/--aat	مصْنوع / ـات	color	lawn/alwaan	ـن / ألْوان

to buy	ishtaraa -- yashtaree	اِشْتَرَى – يَشْتَرِيْ
product	muntaj/--aat	مُنْتج / ات
quality	jawdah	جَوْدة
high	'aalee	عالي
price	si'r/as'aar	سِعْر / أسْعار
cheap	rakheeS	رخيص
to find	wajad -- yajid	وجد – يجد
store, shop	maHall/--aat	محلّ / ات
souk al-Hamidiya*	sooq al-Hameedeeyah	سوق الحميديّة
to ask (for)	sa'al – yas'al ('an)	سأل – يسْأل (عن)
Ask!	is'aloo	إسْألوا
Syria	ash-shaam	الشّام
for, in order to	li	لِـ
The Orient	sharqeeyaat	شَرْقيّات
professor; master	ustaath/asaatithah	أُستاذ / أساتذة
water pipe	narjeelah/--aat	نَرْجيلة / ات
possible; one can	mumkin	مُمْكن
with	ma'	مع
sugar	sukkar	سُكَّر
little	qaleel/--een	قليل / ـين
Have (m) a seat!	ijlis	إجْلِس!
allow me	law samaHt	لَوْ سمحت

yellow	Safraa'	صَفْراء (f)
only	faqaT	فقط
900	tis'amaa'ah	تِسْعمائة
lira (Syr. pound)	layrah/--aat	ليرة / ات
expensive	ghaalee	غالي
to pay	dafa' -- yadfa'	دفع – يدْفع
600	sitt-maa'ah	سِتّمائة
impossible	mustaHeel	مُسْتحيل
take (m)!/get (m)!	khuth	خُذ!
red	Hamraa'	حَمْراء (f)
800	thamaanmaa'ah	ثمانمائة
blue	zarqaa'	زرْقاء (f)
to make	'amil -- ya'mal	عمِل – يعْمل
good	jayyid/--een	جيّد / ـين
for you (m)	laka	لَكَ
for you (f)	laki	لَكِ
700	saba'maa'ah	سبعْمائة
difficult/hard	Sa'b/--een	صعب / ـين
to take	akhath–ya'khuth	أخذ – يأخُذ
congratulations!	mabrook	مبْروك
really	fi'lan	فعلاً
response to God bless you	allaah ybaarik feek	الله يُبارِك فيك

* famous market in Damascus

Grammar القواعد

1. Personal Suffixes with Prepositions 7

In Lesson 2 you already learned the preposition ['ind] عِنْد with the attached personal suffix of *to have*. Personal suffixes are also attached to other prepositions which are the equivalent of the English dative or accusative forms *me, you, him, her*, etc.

	singular			plural		
1st person	with me	maʿee	مَعي	with us	maʿnaa	مَعَنا
2nd person	with you (m)	maʿak	مَعَك	with you	maʿkum	مَعَكُم
	with you (f)	maʿik	مَعِك			
3rd person	with him	maʿhu	مَعَهُ	with them	maʿhum	مَعَهُم
	with her	maʿhaa	مَعَها			

The Alif Maksoora ى [aa] with the prepositions إلى [ilaa] and على [ʿalaa] becomes in connection with the personal suffixes ـَيْ [ay].

up to; to me	ilayya	إلَيَّ	on; to us	ʿalaynaa	عَلَيْنا
up to; to her	ilayhaa	إلَيْها	on; to you (pl)	ʾalaykum	عَلَيْكُم

After the prepositions في [fee], and بِ [bi], إلى [ilaa], على [ʿalaa], the [u] of the personal suffixes of the 3rd person singular (m) and the 3rd person plural become [i] (vocal harmony).

in him	feehi	فيهِ	in; with you (pl)	bihim	بِهِم
up to; to him	ilayhi	إلَيْهِ	on; to them	ʿalayhim	عَلَيْهِم

2. Preposition 6

Like all words that consist of only one letter, the preposition لِ [li] *for* is linked with the word that follows. In addition, the alif of the article الـ [al] is dropped.

for peace	lis-salaam	لِلسَّلام
for the children	lil-aTfaal	لِلأطفال

In connection with personal suffixes, لِ [li] becomes لَ [la]. Only with the suffix of the 1st person singular is it لي [lee] *for me*.

for you (m, sing)	laka	لَكَ	for you (f, sing)	laki	لَكِ
for him	lahu	لَهُ	for you (pl)	lakum	لَكُم

3. Roots and Structures — The Imperative 4, 5

The imperative or command form is made from the 2nd person of the present tense. The prefix ـتَ [ta-] is dropped and replaced by an Alif which is in most cases vocalized with a short i. In addition, the noon (ن) in the ending of the 2nd person singular (f) and the 2nd person plural is dropped.

present tense			imperative		
you (m) sit	tajlis	تَجْلِس	(you, m) sit!	ijlis	إجْلِس
you (f) sit	tajliseen	تَجْلِسين	(you, f) sit!	ijlisee	إجْلِسي
you (pl) sit	tajlisoon	تَجْلِسون	(you, pl) sit!	ijlisoo	إجْلِسوا

Only verbs with a middle vowel (see Lesson 6) in the present tense have a damma (short u), have their alif vocalized with a damma as well.

present tense			imperative		
you (m) write	taktub	تَكْتُب	(you, m) write!	uktub	أُكْتُب
you (f) write	taktubeen	تَكْتُبين	(you, f) write!	uktubee	أُكْتُبي
you (pl) write	taktuboon	تَكْتُبون	(you, pl) write!	uktuboo	أُكْتُبوا

Some verbs form their imperative without alif.

present tense			imperative		
you (m) take	ta'khuth	تَأْخُذ	(you, m) take!	khuth	خُذ
you (f) take	ta'khutheen	تَأْخُذين	(you, f) take!	khuthee	خُذي
you (pl) take	ta'khuthoon	تَأْخُذون	(you, pl) take!	khuthoo	خُذوا

4. Numbers Up to 1000   3

The hundreds are formed with the base number without taa' marbuta (ة) and the word مائة [maa'ah] *hundred*. Both are written in one word. Only *two hundred* uses the dual مائَتَين [maa'atayn].

Numbers from 100 to 1000

100	maa'ah	مائة	600	sitt-maa'ah	سِتّمائة
200	maa'ataynn	مائَتَين	700	sab'a-maa'ah	سَبْعمائة
300	thalaath-maa'ah	ثلاثْمائة	800	thamaan-maa'ah	ثَمانْمائة
400	arba'-maa'ah	أَرْبَعمائة	900	tis'a-maa'ah	تِسْعمائة
500	khams-maa'ah	خَمْسمائة	1000	alf	ألْف

The tens are always connected with و [wa]. In connection with nouns that are always in the singular, taa' marbuta (ة) with مائة [maa'ah] is pronounced. (For rules about nouns with numbers see Lesson 3.)

550	khams-maa'ah wa-khamseen	خَمْسْمائة وخَمْسين
500 lira (Syr. pound)	khams-maa'at layrah	خَمْسْمائة ليرة

Culture Note

Arabic-speaking countries have various currencies. Syria and Lebanon have the lira, and the dirham (دِرْهَم / دراهِم) is the currency in the United Arab Emirates and Morocco. Algiers, Bahrain, Iraq, Jordan, Kuwait, Libya, and Tunisia use the dinar (دينار / دنانير). Qatar, Oman, Saudi Arabia, and Yemen have the riyal (رِيال / ـات) as their currency, while the gineh (جنيه / ـات) is used in Egypt and Sudan.

استعمال اللغة

Usage

Asking for Permission and Apologizing

Allow (m) me	law samaHt	لَوْ سمَحْت
Allow (f) me	law samaHti	لَوْ سمَحْتِ

Excuse me	'afwan	عفْواً
I'm sorry	aasif (ah)	آسِف (ــة)

Shopping 1, 2

I need...	aHtaaj ilaa...	أحْتاج إلى ...
I'm looking for...	abHath 'an...	أبْحث عن ...
Can I see...?	mumkin araa... ?	مُمْكِن أرَىٰ ... ؟
How much (is) that?	bikam haathaa?	بِكَم هٰذا؟
That's too expensive!	haathaa ghaalee jiddan!	هٰذا غالي جداً!
Quote me a good price.	i'mil lee si'r jayyid...	إعْمِل لي سِعْر جيّد!
I'll only pay...	adfa' faqaT...	أدْفع فقط ...
Good, I'll take...	Tayyib, aakhuth...	طيّب ، آخُذ ...
Congratulations!	mabrook	مبْروك!
Response to congratulations (God bless you)	allaah yubaarik feek	الله يُبارِك فيك.

92

Useful Words

عبارات مفيدة أخرى

Roots and Structures — Colors الألوان 3

The following color adjectives have the [if'al] أفْعَل, structure. The structure for the feminine form is [fa'laa] فَعْلاء.

	masculine		feminine			masculine		feminine	
red	aHmar	أحْمَر	Hamraa'	حَمْراء	black	aswad	أسْوَد	sawdaa'	سَوْداء
green	akhDar	أخْضَر	khaDraa'	خَضْراء	white	abyaD	أبْيَض	bayDaa'	بَيْضاء
blue	azraq	أزْرَق	zarqaa'	زَرْقاء	brown, maroon	asmar	أسْمَر	samraa'	سَمْراء
yellow	aSfar	أصْفَر	Safraa'	صَفْراء	blond	ashqar	أشْقَر	shaqraa'	شَقْراء

 Regional Variations

في العامية

Do you have... / Is there...?

In non-Standard Arabic, the preposition [fee] في with the personal suffix of the 3rd person singular *(m)* is used to express *there is* or *I/we have*.

	Syrian		Egyptian	
Is/Are there...?	feeh...?	فيه...؟	feeh...?	فيه...؟
Yes, there is/there are.	iyh, feeh	إيه ، فيه.	aah, feeh	آه ، فيه.
No, there isn't/there aren't.	laa, maa feeh	لا ، ما فيه.	laa, maa feesh	لا ، ما فيش.

Regional Vocabulary

	Syrian	Egyptian
to look (for)	dawwar -- yidawwar ('alaa)	dawwar -- yidawwar ('alaa)
thing, item	shee/ashyaa or shaghlah/--aat	Haagah/--aat
water pipe	argeelah/araageel	sheeshah/shiyash
a little	shwayyah	shwayyah
to sit	a'ad -- yu'ud	a'ad -- yu'ud
How much is...?	bi-addaysh...?	bi-kam...?
very	kteer	giddan or awee
only	bas	bas
a good price	si'r mneeH	si'r kwayyis

ok; alright	maasheel-Haal	maashee
really	'an jad	bi-gad

Exercises التمارين

1 Write a dialogue using the sentences on the right. The first line has already been done for you.

1. ...... لو سمحت ، أبحث عن طاولة. .. — الله يبارك فيك!
2. .... — بكم هٰذه؟
3. .... — تفضّل ، عندي طاولات كثيرة.
4. .... — مبروك!
5. .... — بستّمائة ليرة.
6. .... — لو سمحت ، أبحث عن طاولة.
7. .... — طيّب ، آخذ الطاولة.

2 Are you looking for something or would you like to ask for something? Transform the sentences from the 2nd person plural into the 1st person singular as shown in the example.

1. .. أحتاج إلىٰ هدية. .... — تحتاجون إلىٰ هدية.
2. .... — تبحثون عن محلّ.
3. .... — تسألون عن الأسعار.

3 Listen to the dialogue again and answer the questions as shown in the example.

1. ..بتسعمائة ليرة............................ — بكم النرجيلة الصفراء؟
2. .... — بكم النرجيلة الحمراء؟
3. .... — بكم النرجيلة الزرقاء؟
4. .... — كم يدفع أحمد للنرجيلة الزرقاء؟

4 Using the imperative, speak first to a man then to a woman. Transform the plural imperatives into the singular (m) and (f) forms as shown in the example.

1. .... إذهب إلىٰ اليسار! .. — إذهبوا إلىٰ اليسار! 2. .. إذهبي إلىٰ اليسار! ....
3. .... — إجلسوا هنا! 4. ....
5. .... — إشربوا شاي! 6. ....

94

5 Transform these sentences into the imperative form as shown in the example.

1. تعمل لي سعر جيّد. .. إعمل لي سعر جيّد! ....
2. تسأل عن أبو سعيد. ....
3. تأخذ الحزام الأسود. ....
4. تجلسين جنب الشبّاك. ....
5. تكتبين رسالة. ....

6 Match the personal suffix and its preposition with the appropriate personal pronoun as shown in the example.

1. فيهم   a.   أنا
2. معكم   b.   أنت
3. لي   c.   هو
4. مقابله   d.   هي
5. جنبها   e.   نحن
6. إلينا   f.   أنتم
7. عليك   g.   هم

7 Replace the underlined words with the correct personal suffix of the preposition as shown in the example.

1. نحتاج إلىٰ <u>تاكسي</u>. .. نحتاج إليه. ....
2. المفتاح علىٰ <u>الطاولة</u>. ....
3. تبحثون عن <u>بيت</u>. ....
4. كنت عند <u>أصدقائي</u>. ....
5. يسأل عن <u>الطبيب</u>. ....
6. ذهب إلىٰ <u>السوق</u>. ....

الدرس الثامن

In this lesson you will learn:
- **Food items**
- **Ordering in a restaurant**
- **Personal suffixes with verbs**
- **Verbs with basic stems**
- **Verbs with VIII stems**
- **Negatives in regular sentences**

سلطة تبولة

المقادير:

٤ ملاعق كبيرة زيت زيتون	حزمة نعناع	نصف كأس برغل
ملح	حزمتين بقدونس	ماء
فلفل أسود	حبة طماطم كبيرة	عصير ليمونتين
خسّ للزينة	نصف خيارة	٣ بصلات

الطريقة:

نغسل البرغل وننقعه لمدّة ساعة في الماء ، ثمّ نصفيه وبعد ذلك نضيف إليه عصير الليمون ونضعه جانباً. نقطع البقدونس والنعناع والخضر ونضيفها مع الزيت والبهارات إلىٰ البرغل ، ثمّ نقدّم السلطة علىٰ أوراق الخسّ في صحن.

Tabbouleh-Salad

Measurements:

½ glass of bulgur	1 bunch of mint	4 tablespoons of olive oil
water	2 bunches of parsley	salt
juice of 2 lemons	1 large tomato	black pepper
3 onions	½ cucumber	green lettuce (for decoration)

Preparation:

Wash the bulgur* and soak it in water for one hour. Drain it, add lemon juice and set it aside. Cut the parsley, the mint, and the vegetables and add it with the oil to the bulgur. Serve the salad on lettuce leaves on a plate.

* bulgur is a quick cooking form of wheat

What's New? ما الجديد؟

Personal suffixes are not only attached to nouns and prepositions (see Lesson 7), but also to verbs. Here they function as objects similar to the English pronouns *him, her, it, them*, etc.

We put <u>the bulgur</u> to the side.	naDa' al-burghul jaaniban	نضع البُرْغُل جانِباً.
We put <u>it</u> to the side.	naDa'hu jaaniban	نضعهُ جانِباً.

We add <u>the vegetables</u> to <u>the bulgur</u>.	nuDiif al-khuDar ilaa al-burghul	نُضيف الخُضر إلى البُرْغُل.
We add <u>them</u> to <u>it</u>.	nuDiifhaa ilayhi	نُضيفها إليْهِ.

fee al-maT'am في المطعم

Mahmood and Samirah are sitting in a restaurant waiting for Ahmad, who seems to be late.

sameerah:	anaa jaw'aanah. hal naTlub al-akl aw nantaTHir Ahmad?	سميرة: أنا جوعانة. هل نطلب الأكل أو ننتظر أحمد؟
maHmood:	nantaTHirh qaleelan.	محمود: ننتظره قليلاً.
aHmad:	masaa' al-khayr yaa shabaab! … anaa aasif 'alaa at-ta'kheer. hal Talabtum?	أحمد: مساء الخير يا شباب! … أنا آسف على التأخير. هل طلبتم؟
sameerah:	laa, intaTHarnaak. maathaa na'kul?	سميرة: لا ، انتظرناك. ماذا نأكل؟
aHmad:	laa a'rif. maathaa tureedoon?	أحمد: لا أعرف. ماذا تريدون؟
maHmood:	anaa ureed as-salaTah wa shoorbat al-'adis wa ad-dajaaj ma' ar-ruz.	محمود: أنا أريد السلطة وشوربة العدس والدجاج مع الرزّ.
sameerah:	haathihi fikrah jayyidah. laakin laa uHibb al-'adis.	سميرة: هذه فكرة جيدة. لكن لا أحبّ العدس.
maHmood:	yaa sayyidee!	محمود: يا سيّدي!
al-jarsoon:	masaa' al-khayr! hal taTluboon al-'ashaa'.	الجرسون: مساء الخير! هل تطلبون العشاء؟
maHmood:	na'am, na'khuth as-salaTah wa shoorbat al-khuDar wa ad-dajaaj ma' ar-ruz.	محمود: نعم ، نأخذ السلطة وشوربة الخضر والدجاج مع الرزّ.
al-jarsoon:	wa maathaa tashraboon?	الجرسون: وماذا تشربون؟ فيه كولا وعصير فواكه و…
	feeh koolaa wa 'aSeer fawaakih wa….	

maHmood:	koolaa, min faDlak.	كولا ، من فضلك.	محمود:
al-jarsoon:	tafaDDaloo, biS-SaHah.	تفضّلوا ، بالصحّة!	الجرسون:
sameerah:	law samaHt, maa Talabnaa shoorbat al-ʿadis, Talabnaa shoorbat al-khuDar.	لو سمحت ، ما طلبنا شوربة العدس ، طلبنا شوربة الخضر.	سميرة:
al-jarsoon:	anaa aasif. aHDarhaa fawran.	أنا آسف. أحضرها فوراً.	الجرسون:
maHmood:	yaa akh! al-Hisaab, min faDlak.	يا أخ! الحساب ، من فضلك.	محمود:
aHmad:	laa, laa! anaa adfaʿ haathihi al-marrah.	لا ، لا! أنا أدفع هٰذه المرّة.	أحمد:
maHmood:	laa, wal-laah! al-Hisaab ʿalayya.	لا ، والله! الحساب عليّ.	محمود:

Vocabulary المفردات

From this lesson on, the stem of a verb is indicated with a Roman numeral in front of it. Verbs with basic stems do not have a numeral.

salad	salaTah/--aat	سلطة / ـات	cucumbers	khiyaar	خيار
Tabbouleh (salad with a lot of parsley)	tabboolih	تبّولة	spoon	milʿaqah/malaaʿiq	ملْعقة / ملاعِق
Measurement	miqdaar/maqaadeer	مِقْدار / مقادير	oil	zayt	زَيْت
glass	kaʾs/kuʾoos	كأس / كؤوس	olives	zaytoon	زَيتون
bulgur	burghul	بُرْغُل	salt	milH	مِلح
water	maaʾ	ماء	black pepper	filfil aswad	فِلفِل أسْود
juice	ʿaSeer	عصير	lettuce	khass	خسّ
lemons	laymoon	لَيْمون	decoration	zeenah	زينة
onions	baSal	بصل	preparation	Tareeqah	طريقة
bunch	Hizmah	حِزْمة	to wash	ghasal -- yaghsil	غسل – يغْسِل
mint	naʿnaaʿ	نعْناع	to soak	naqaʿ -- yanqaʿ	نقع – ينْقع
parsley	baqdoonis	بقْدونِس	duration	muddah	مُدّة
piece	Habbah	حبّة	for an hour	limuddat saaʿah	لِمُدّة ساعة
tomatoes	TamaaTim	طماطِم	then	thumma	ثُمّ

to drain	Saffaa -- yuSaffee	صَفّىٰ – يُصَفّي
to add	aDaaf -- yuDeef (ilaa)	VI أضاف – يُضيف (إلىٰ)
to put	waDa' -- yaDa'	وضع – يضع
aside	jaaniban	جانباً
to cut	qaTa' -- yaqTa'	قطع – يقْطع
vegetables	khuDar	خُضر
to serve	bihaaraat	بهارات
to present	qaddam – yuqaddim (li)	II قدّم – يُقدّم (لِـ)
leaf	waraq/awraaq	ورق / أوْراق
plate	SaHin/SuHoon	صحْن / صُحون
hungry	jaw'aan/--een	جوْعان / ـــين
to order	Talab -- yaTlub	طلب – يطْلُب
food; meal	akl/--aat	أكل / ـــات
to wait (for)	intaTHar -- yantaTHir	VIII انْتظر – ينْتظِر
I'm sorry (for)	anaa aasif ('alaa)	أنا آسِف (علىٰ)
delay	ta'kheer	تأخير
(in front of verbs in the present tense) not	laa	لا
to eat	akal -- ya'kul	أكل – يأْكُل
to like, to want	araad -- yureed	VI أراد – يُريد

soup	shoorbah	شورْبة
lentils	'adiss	عدس
chicken	dajaaj	دجاج
rice	ruzz	رُزّ
idea	fikrah / afkaar	فِكْرة / أفْكار
to like, to love	aHabb -- yuHibb	VI أحبّ – يُحِبّ
to prefer	faDDal -- yufaDDil	II فضّل – يُفضّل
waiter	jarsoon	جرْسون
dinner	'ashaa'	عشاء
(slang) there is; we have	feeh	فيه
cola	koolaa	كولا
fruit	fawaakih	فواكِه
here you (pl) are	tafaDDaloo	تفضّلوا
Enjoy your meal!	biS-SaHHah	بالصّحّة!
past tense negation prefix	maa	ما
to bring	aHDar -- yuHDir	VI أحْضر – يُحْضِر
Brother! (address for a stranger)	yaa akh	يا أخ!
bill	Hisaab/--aat	حِساب / ـــات
this time	haathihi al-marrah	هٰذِه المرّة
This (is) on me.	al-Hisaab 'alayya	الحِساب عليَّ.

99

Culture Note

In coffee shops and restaurants in the Arabic speaking world, separate bills are uncommon. In the Arab culture you show your generosity by insisting on paying the bill. Hospitality is of utmost importance and the person invited will try to pay the bill. Young people usually split the bill.

Grammar القواعد

1. Roots and Structures – Basic Stem   5, 4

Verbs in Arabic are formed by using various structures: double consonants, vowel stretching, prefixes, or a combination of these. There are ten different patterns of vowel stems. In dictionaries or grammar reference, you will often find them under their roots identified by Roman numerals.

You already know many verbs with their basic stem and the structure فَعَل – يَـفْعَل [faʿal -- yafʿal] . The verbs [saʾal – yasʾal] سأل – يسأل to ask and [dafaʿ -- yadfaʿ] دفع – يدْفع to pay follow the same structure, their root is [s-ʾ-l] (س – ء – ل) and [d-f-ʿ] (د – ف – ع).

past tense			present tense		
I asked; you (m) asked	saʾalt saʾalt	سَأَلْـت	I ask	asʾal	سْأَل
she asked	saʾalat	سَأَلَـت	you (m) ask; she asks	tasʾal tasʾal	تَـسْأَل
they asked	saʾaloo	سَأَلـوا	they ask	yasʾaloon	يَـسْأَلـون

past tense			present tense		
I paid; you (m) paid	dafaʿt dafaʿt	دَفَعْـت	I pay	adfaʿ	أدْفَع
she paid	dafaʿat	دَفَعَـت	you (m) pay; she pays	tadfaʿ tadfaʿ	تَـدْفَع
they paid	dafaʿoo	دَفَعـوا	they pay	yadfaʿoon	يَـدْفَعـون

2. Roots and Structures – Stem VIII 4

The structure of stem VIII is اِفْتَعَل – يَفْتَعِل [ifta'al -- yafta'il]. Note that there is no vowel in the first root consonant and تَـ [-ta-] is added after the first root consonant. The verbs اِشْتَغَل – يِشْتَغِل [ishtaghal -- yashtaghil] *to work* and اِنْتَظَر – يِنْتَظِر [intaTHar -- yantaTHir] *to wait* have stem VIII. You find them in the dictionary under the root (ش – غ – ل) [sh-'-l] and (ن – ظ – ر) [n-TH-r].

past tense			present tense		
I worked; you (m) have worked	ishtaghalt ishtaghalt	اِشْتَغَلْت	I work	ashtaghil	أَشْتَغِل
she worked	ishtaghalat	اِشْتَغَلَت	you (m) work; she works	tashtaghil tashtaghil	تَـشْتَغِل
they worked	ishtaghaloo	اِشْتَغَلوا	they work	yashtaghiloon	يَـشْتَغِلون

past tense			present tense		
I waited; you (m) waited	intaTHart intaTHart	اِنْتَظَرْت	I wait	antaTHir	أَنْتَظِر
she waited	intaTHarat	اِنْتَظَرَت	you (m) wait; she waits	tantaTHir tantaTHir	تَـنْتَظِر
they waited	intaTHaroo	اِنْتَظَروا	they wait	yantaTHiroon	يَـنْتَظِرون

The verbs [ishtaraa -- yashtaree] اِشْتَرى – يِشْتَري *to buy* and اِحْتاج – يِحْتاج [iHtaaj -- yaHtaaj] *to need* are stem VIII verbs. Since the weak root consonants ي [y] and و [w] can either turn into a diphthong or a vowel, or disappear altogether, it is sometimes difficult to determine what the root is. The roots are (ش – ر – ي) [sh-r-y] and (ح – و – ج) [H-w-j].

to buy		اِشْتَرى – يِشْتَري	to need		اِحْتاج – يِحْتاج
I buy	ashtaree	أَشْتَري	I need	aHtaaj	أَحْتاج
you (m) buy; she buys	tashtaree tashtaree	تَـشْتَري	you (m) need; she needs	taHtaaj taHtaaj	تَـحْتاج
they buy	yashtaroon	يَـشْتَرون	they need	yaHtaajoon	يَـحْتاجون

You will find a summary of all 10 verb stems in the grammar guide at www.berlitzbooks.com/basicarabic.

3. Personal Suffixes with Verbs   3

The verb اِنْتَظَر — يَنْتَظِر [intaTHar -- yantaTHir] *to wait* doesn't require a preposition as it does in the English *to wait (for)*. Therefore, personal suffixes are attached directly to the verb. The personal suffix of the 1st person singular in connection with verbs is ـني [-nee].

you waited	intaTHart	اِنْتَظَرْت	→	*you waited for me*	intaTHartnee	اِنْتَظَرْتَني
I wait	antaTHir	أَنْتَظِر	→	*I wait for you (m)*	antaTHirak	أَنْتَظِرَك
she waited	intaTHarat	اِنْتَظَرَت	→	*she waited for him*	intaTHarathu	اِنْتَظَرَتْهُ
he waits	yantaTHir	يَنْتَظِر	→	*he waits for her*	yantaTHirhaa	يَنْتَظِرْها

In the past tense form of the 2nd person plural, a Waw (و) is inserted. In the 3rd person plural the personal suffix is added and the Alif of the ending [--oo] ـوا is dropped.

you (pl) waited	intaTHartum	اِنْتَظَرْتم	→	*you waited for us*	intaTHartumoonaa	اِنْتَظَرْتُمونا
they waited	intaTHaroo	اِنْتَظَروا	→	*they waited for you*	intaTHarookum	اِنْتَظَروكُم

In the present tense, if a personal suffix is added to the 2nd person singular (f) and the 2nd and 3rd person plural forms, the noon (ن) of the ending is dropped.

you (f) wait	tantaTHireen	تَنْتَظِرين	→	*you (f) wait for us*	tantaTHireenaa	تَنْتَظِرينا
you (pl) wait	tantaTHiroon	تَنْتَظِرون	→	*you (pl) wait for them*	tantaTHiroohum	تَنْتَظِروهُم

4. Negatives in Regular Sentences   7

In the past tense, verbs are negated with [maa] ما, and in the present tense with [laa] لا.

We did not order this.	maa Talabnaa haathaa	ما طلَبْنا هٰذا.
I don't know.	laa a'rif	لا أعْرِف.
I don't like lentils.	laa uHibb al-'adis	لا أُحِبّ العدس.

Usage   استعمال اللغة

Expressing Likes and Dislikes   6

I don't like soup.	laa uHibb ash-shoorbah	لا أُحِبّ الشّورْبة.
I prefer salad.	ufaDDil as-salaTah	أُفضّل السَّلطة.

Ordering in a Restaurant   8

Waiter! (lit. sir; brother)	yaa sayyidee!/yaa akh!	يا سيِّدي! / يا أخ!
Are you ready to order dinner?	hal taTluboon al-'ashaa'?	هل تطْلُبون العشاء؟
We will have chicken with rice.	na'khuth ad-dajaaj ma' ar-ruzz	نأخُذ الدّجاج مع الرُّزّ.
What will you have to drink?	wa maathaa tashraboon	وماذا تشْربون؟
Water, please.	maa', min faDlak	ماء ، مِن فضْلك.
Here you are. Enjoy your meal.	tafaDDaloo, biS-SaHHah!	تفضّلوا ، بالصَّحّة!
The bill, please.	al-Hisaab, min FaDlak	الحِساب ، مِن فضْلك.

Useful Words

4. Food Items *1, 2*

عبارات مفيدة أخرىٰ

Many food items are collective nouns. These are nouns that denote a group of individual people or items in the plural. The singular is formed by adding The taa' marbuta (ة).

lemons (coll)	laymoon	لَيْمون	onions (coll)	baSal	بَصل
one lemon	laymoonah	لَيْمونة	one onion	baSalah	بَصلة

fruit	**al-fawaakih**	الفَواكِه	**vegetables**	**al-khuDar**	الخُضر
apples	tuffaaH	تُفّاح (coll.)	potatoes	baTaaTaa	بطاطا (coll.)
oranges	burtuqaal	بُرْتُقال (coll.)	eggplant	baathinjaan	باذِنْجان (coll.)
grapes	'anab	عنب (coll.)	zucchini	koosaa	كوسَى (coll.)
melons	baTTeekh	بطّيخ (coll.)	green peppers	filfil	فِلفِل (coll.)
bananas	mawz	مَوْز (coll.)	carrots	jazar	جزر (coll.)

breakfast	**al-fuToor**	الفُطور	**lunch**	**al-ghadaa'**	الغَداء
milk	Haleeb	حليب (f)	beef (meat)	laHm baqr	لحْم بَقْر
bread	khubz	خُبْز (coll.)	lamb (meat)	laHm ghanam	لحْم غَنم
butter	zubd	زُبْد (coll.)	fish	samak	سمك (coll.)
cheese	jubn	جُبْن (coll.)	kebob	kabaab	كباب
eggs	bayD	بَيْض (coll.)	gyros	shawarmah	شوَرمة

في العامية

Regional Variations

Negative Forms in Simple Non-Standard Arabic Sentences

To express the negative form a sentence in Syrian Arabic, use ما [maa]. In Egyptian Arabic, add the ending ـش [-sh].

	Syrian		Egyptian	
we didn't order	maa Talabnaa	ما طلبْنا	maa talabnaash	ما طلبْناش
I don't know	maa baaʿrif	ما باعْرِف	maa aʿrafsh	ما أعْرَفْـش
I don't like	maa biHibb	ما بِحِبّ	maa baHibbish	ما بَحِبّـش

Regional Vocabulary

	Syrian	Egyptian
or	wallaa	wallaa
to wait	istannaa -- yistannaa	istannaa - yistannaa
to want, to like	bidd + personal suffix	ʿaawiz/--een, ʿaayiz /--een
chicken	dajaaj	firaakh
That's a good idea.	hay fikrah mneeHah	dee fikrah Hilwah
but	bass	laakin or bass
Enjoy your meal.	saHTayn!	bil-hanaa wash-shifaa!
to bring	jaab -- yijeeb	gaab -- yigeeb

105

## Exercises	التمارين

1 Read the recipe on the first page of this lesson again. Mark which ingredients you need for a tabbouleh salad.

7. عدس ☐		4. خيار ☐		1. بقدونس ☒
8. ليمون ☐		5. طماطم ☐		2. باذنجان ☐
9. نعناع ☐		6. جزر ☐		3. بصل ☐

2 One word doesn't fit in the row. Mark it.

ماء ☒	موز ☐	بطيخ ☐	1. عنب ☐
عشاء ☐	غداء ☐	فواكه ☐	2. فطور ☐
دجاج ☐	لحم بقر ☐	خبز ☐	3. لحم غنم ☐
بيض ☐	صحن ☐	ملعقة ☐	4. كأس ☐

3 Replace the underlined words with the appropriate personal suffix as shown in the example. Keep in mind that plurals that do not relate to persons are treated like feminine singulars.

1. انتظر <u>صديقه</u>. انتظره. ....
2. أكل <u>الشوربة</u>. ....
3. درس <u>لغات كثيرة</u>. ....
4. سأل <u>السيّدة</u> عن الطريق. ....

4 Change these sentences in the 1st person singular into the present tense form as shown in the example.

1. شربت كأس ماء. أشرب كأس ماء. ....
2. كتبت رسائل. ....
3. اشتريت فواكه. ....
4. دفعت الحساب. ....

5 Change these sentences in the 2nd person singular into the past tense form as shown in the example.

1. تأخذ السمك والرزّ. .. أخذت السمك والرزّ.
2. تعرف الطريق إلى المتحف. ....
3. تسكن في بلد عربي. ....
4. تفهم الإنكليزية؟ ....

6 You don't like soup and prefer salad instead? Play your role as shown in the example.

1. شوربة – سلطة .. لا أحبّ الشوربة ، أفضّل السلطة.
2. قهوة – شاي ....
3. كولا – عصير ....
4. تفّاح – برتقال ....

7 Put these sentences in the 1st person plural into the negative as shown in the example.

ما	لا	ما	لا
1. جلسنا في المطعم.	ما	3. نريد طاولة جنب الشبّاك.	....
2. طلبنا العشاء.	....	4. نشتغل في يوم السبت.	....

8 You and your friends are sitting in a restaurant. Do the following:

1. Call the waiter. .. يا سيّدي! ....
2. Order lamb with potatoes. ....
3. Tell the waiter that you didn't order rice, but potatoes. ....
4. Ask for the check. ....

الدرس التاسع
9

In this lesson you will learn:
- **To Congratulate**
- **To Introduce Family members**
- **Stem IV verbs**
- **Negatives in regular sentences**
- **Weak verbs**
- **Indirect speech**

عيد مبارك!

الصديق العزيز أحمد وعائلته الكريمة
أرسل إليكم أطيب التحيات بمناسبة عيد الفطر المبارك.
أتمنّى أن تصلكم هذه الرسالة وأنتم في أحسن حال.
كلّ سنة وأنتم بخير!
صديقكم المخلص
توماس

Happy Holidays!
To my dear friend Ahmad and his generous Family!
I'm sending you my warmest greetings for Ramadan. I hope that this letter will reach you in the best of health.
All the best!
Your sincere friend,
Thomas

ما الجديد؟ / What's New?

1. Roots and Structures — Stem IV 5, 8

The verb IV stem has the structure أَفْعَل — يُـفْعِل [af'al -- yuf'il]. You'll recognize it by the prefix [a-] and the absence of the vowel of the first root consonant. The present tense form begins with يُـ [yu-].

أَرْسَل — يُرْسِل [arsal -- yursil] *to send* and أَحَبّ — يُحِبّ [aHabb – yuHibb] *to love, to like* are verbs with the IV stem, their roots being (ح – ب – ب) [h-b-b] and (ر – س – ل) [r-s-l].

past tense			present tense		
I sent; you (m) sent	arsalt arsalt	أَرْسَلْـتُ	I send	ursil	أُرْسِل
she sent	arsalat	أَرْسَلَـتْ	you (m) send; she sends	tursil tursil	تُـرْسِل
they sent	arsaloo	أَرْسَلُـوا	they send	yursiloon	يُـرْسِلـون

past tense			present tense		
I loved; you (m) loved	aHbabt aHbabt	أَحْبَبْـتُ	I love	uHibb	أُحِبّ
she loved	aHabbat	أَحَبَّـتْ	you (m) love; she loves	tuHibb tuHibb	تُـحِبّ
they loved	aHabboo	أَحَبُّـوا	they love	yuHibboon	يُـحِبّـون

 ramaDaan kareem! رمضان كريم!

Thomas is visiting Ahmad's family during Ramadan.
toomaas yazoor 'aailat Ahmad fee ramaDaan.

توماس يزور عائلة أحمد في رمضان.

toomaas: as-salaam 'alaykum! ramaDaan Kareem!

توماس: السلام عليكم! رمضان كريم!

Ahmad: wa 'alayk as-salaam! tafaDDal, udkhul! kayf Haalak?

أحمد: وعليك السلام! تفضّل، أدخل، كيف حالك؟

toomaas: al-Hamdu lil-laah, anaa bikhayr. tafaDDal, haathihi hadeeyah Sagheerah, Halaweeyaat lil-'aa'ilah.

توماس: الحمد لله، أنا بخير. تفضّل، هذه هدية صغيرة، حلويات للعائلة.

Ahmad: shukran jazeelan.

أحمد: شكراً جزيلاً.

yadkhuloon al-ghurfah, hunaak akhoo Ahmad.

دخلون الغرفة، هناك أخو أحمد.

Ahmad: ijlus yaa toomaas haathaa akhee kareem. a'Tee umee al-Halaweeyaat. hiya fee al-maTbakh wa taTbukh al-akal ma' ukhtee.

أحمد: إجلس يا توماس! هذا أخي كريم. أعطي أمي الحلويات. هي في المطبخ وتطبخ الأكل مع أختي.

Ahmad yakhraj min al-ghurfah.

أحمد يخرج من الغرفة.

kareem: akhee qaal lee innak Tabeeb. anaa ayDan ureed an adrus aT-Tib.

كريم: أخي قال لي إنّك طبيب. أنا أيضاً أريد أن أدرس الطبّ.

toomaas: haathihi fikrah mumtaazah. al-mustashfayaat taHtaaj ilaa aTibbaa' jayyideen.

توماس: هذه فكرة ممتازة. المستشفيات تحتاج إلى أطبّاء جيّدين.

109

٩

أحمد وأبوه يرجعون.

Ahmad wa abooh yarja'oon.

Ahmad:	toomaas, haathaa abee. baabaa, haathaa Sadeeqee toomaas.	توماس ، هٰذا أبي. بابا ، هذا صديقي توماس.
aboo Ahmad:	ahlan wa sahlan! marHaban bik 'indnaa! hal anta jaw'aan?	أهلاً وسهلاً! مرحباً بك عندنا! هل أنت جوعان؟
toomaas:	laa, anaa shab'aan. wa laakin antum Saa'imeen minthu aS-SabaaH.	لا ، أنا شبعان. ولٰكن أنتم صائمين منذ الصباح.
aboo Ahmad:	lasnaa jaw'aaneen jiddan, wa laakin aqool lak: naHnu 'aTshaneen!	لسنا جوعانين جدّاً ، ولٰكن أقول لك: نحن عطشانين!

Tadkhul um Ahmad wa ukhtuh wa bintahaa aS-Sagheerah.

تدخل أمّ أحمد وأخته وبنتها الصغيرة.

Ahmad:	haathihi ummee wa hathihi ukhtee faaTimah. wa haathihi naadiyah, binthaa, 'umrhaa thalaath sanawaat. ta'aalee yaa naadiyah, qoolee marHaban li-'am toomaas!	هذه أمّي وهٰذه أختي فاطمة. وهذه نادية ، بنتها ، عمرها ثلاث سنوات. تعالي يا نادية ، قولي مرحباً لعمّ توماس!
umm Ahmad:	bis-millaah, nabda' al-ifTaar. tafaDDal yaa toomaas, khuth at-tamr wa al-Haleeb!	بسم الله ، نبدأ الإفطار. تفضّل يا توماس ، خذ التمر والحليب!
aboo Ahmad:	bil-SaHHah.	بالصحّة!

المفردات

dear	'azeez/a'izzaa'	عزيز / أعزّاء
generous	kareem/kiraam	كريم / كِرام
to send (to)	arsal -- yursil (ilaa)	IV أرسل – يُرسِل (إلى)
best; dearest	aTyab	TK
greeting	taHayyah/--aat	تحيّة / ات
occasion	munaasabah/--aat	مُناسبة / ات
feast day	'eed/a'yaad	عيد / أعياد
feast celebrating end of Ramadan	'eed al-fiTr	عيد الفِطر
blessed	mubaarak	مُبارك
to hope	tamannaa-yatamannaa	تمنّى – يتمنّى
I hope (that) ...	atamannaa an...	أتمنّى أن ...
to arrive;	waSal--yaSil	وصل – يصِل
best	aHsan	أحسن
All the best!	kull sanah wa antum bi-khayr	كل سنة وأنتم بخير!

sincere; honest	mukhliS/--een	مُخْلِص / ــين
to visit	zaar -- yazoor	زار – يزور
Ramadan	ramaDaan	رمضان
to enter; to come in	dakhal -- yadkhul	دخل – يدْخُل
sweets	Halaweeyaat	حلويّات
brother	akh/ikhwah	أخ / إخوة
to give	a'Taa -- yu'Tee	IV أعْطَى – يُعْطي
mother	umm/ummahaat	أُمّ (f) / أُمّهات
to cook	Tabakh -- yaTbukh	طبخ – يطْبُخ
sister	ukht/akhawaat	أُخْت (f) / أخَوات
to walk out (of)	kharaj -- yakhruj (min)	خرج – يخْرُج (مِن)
to say (to s.o.)	qaal – yaqool (li)	قال – يقول (لِ)
to say that ...	qaal inna...	قال إنَّ ...
that you (m)	innaka	إنّك
medicine	Tibb	طب
to like (to do) s.th.	araad -- yureed an (yaf'al)	IV أراد – يُريد أنْ (يفْعل)

also	ayDan	أيْضاً
to return (to)	raja' -- yarji' (ilaa)	رجع – يرْجع (إلى)
father	ab/aaba'	أب / آباء
dad	baabaa	بابا
full	shab'aan/--een	شبْعان / ــين
fasting person	Saa'im/--een	صائِم / ــين
thirsty	'aTshaan/--een	عطْشان / ــين
Come (f) here!	ta'aalee	تعالي
Say! (f)	qoolee	قولي
Uncle, paternal	'amm	عمّ
in the name of God	bis-mil-laah	بِسْم الله
to begin; to start	bada' -- yabda'	بدأ – يبْدأ
breaking the fast; breakfast	ifTaar	إفْطار
dates	tamr	تَمْر (coll.)

القواعد

Grammar

1. Roots and Structures — Weak Verbs 9, 8, 6

In Lessons 4–8 you learned about verbs with their weak root consonants و [w] or ي [y]. These consonants are often not identifiable because in conjugation, their diphthongs or vowels disappear. In this lesson you'll learn about verbs where the changes of weak root consonants are easily recognizable. Try to memorize these conjugations. The more examples you know, the easier it will be to conjugate similar verbs.

The verb وصل – يصل [waSal -- yaSil] *to arrive* has in its basic stem the root (و – ص – ل) [w-S-l].
The weak root consonant و [w] is dropped in the present tense.

Similar verbs: وضع – يضع [waDa' – yaDa'] *to put;* وجد – يجِد [wajad -- yajid] *to find;* وقع – يقع [waqa' – yaqa'] *to fall;* وقف – يقِف [waqaf -- yaqif] *to stop*

past tense			present tense		
I arrived; you (m) arrived	waSalt waSalt	وَصَلْـت	I arrive	aSil	صِل
she arrived	waSalat	وَصَلَـت	you (m) arrive; she arrives	taSil taSil	ـصِل
they arrived	waSaloo	وَصَلـوا	they arrive	yaSiloon	ـصِلـون

The verb أراد – يُريد [araad -- yureed] *to want, to like* has in its IV stem the root (ر – و – د) [r-w-d]. The weak root consonant becomes [a], [aa] and [ee].

Similar verb: أضاف – يُضيف [aDaaf -- yuDeef] *to add*

past tense			present tense		
I wanted; you (m) wanted	aradt aradt	أَرَدْت	I'd like	ureed	ريد
she wanted	araadat	أَرادَت	you (m) would like; she'd like	tureed tureed	ـريد
they wanted	araadoo	أَرادوا	they'd like	yureedoon	ـريدون

To express that someone intends to do something, use أراد – يُريد [araad -- yureed] and the conjunction أنْ [an] *that,* to which the present tense verb construction is connected. Both verbs have to be conjugated.

| My brother wants to study medicine. (lit. My brother wants that he studies medicine.) | akhee yureed an yadrus aT-Tibb | خي يُريد أنْ يدْرُس الطِّبّ. |
| I wanted to go to the movies. (lit. I wanted that I go to the movies.) | aradt an athhab ilaa as-seenimaa | رَدْت أنْ أذهب إلى السّينما. |

112

The verb أَعْطَى – يُعْطِي [aʿTaa – yuʿTee] *to give* has in its IV stem the root (ع – ط – و) [ʿ-T-w]. The weak root consonant becomes [ai], [a], [au] and [ee] or is dropped altogether.

Similar verb: اِشْتَرَى – يَشْتَرِي [ishtaraa -- yashtiree] *to buy*

past tense			present tense		
I gave;	aʿTayt	أَعْطَيْتُ	I give	uʿTee	أُعْطِي
you (m) gave	aʿTayt		you (m) give; she gives	tuʿTee tuʿTee	تُعْطِي
she gave	aʿTat	أَعْطَتْ			
they gave	aʿTaw	أَعْطَوْا	they give	yuʿToon	يُعْطُونَ

The verb قال – يقول [qaal -- yaqool] *to say* has in its basic stem the root (ق – و – ل) [q-w-l]. The weak root consonant becomes [aa], [o], [oo], and [ee].

Similar verbs: زار – يزور [zaar -- yazoor] *to visit*; كان – يكون [kaan -- yakoon] *to be* as well the dialect verbs راح – يروح [raaH -- yarooH] *to go* and شاف – يشوف [shaaf -- yashoof] *to see*.

past tense			present tense		
I said;	qult	قُلْتُ	I say	aqool	أَقُول
you (m) said	qult		you (m) say; she says	taqool taqool	تَقُول
she said	qaalat	قَالَتْ			
they said	qaaloo	قَالُوا	they say	yaqooloon	يَقُولُونَ

2. Indirect Speech   3

Indirect speech is formed with the verb قال – يقول [qaal -- yaqool] and the conjunction إنَّ [inna] *that*, which is always followed by a noun or personal suffix, not a verb.

They say that the train has arrived.	yaqooloon inna al-qiTaar waSal	يقولون إنّ القطار وصل.
He told me that you are a doctor.	qaal lee innak Tabeeb	قال لي إنّك طبيب.

Usage

Congratulations 1

Whether it's someone's birthday or it's New Year's Eve, this phrase can be used for all annual occasions! كُلّ سنة وأنْتُم بخَيْر [kull sanah wa antum bi-khayr] *Be well every year!* The proper response is وأنْتَ بخَيْر [wa anta bi-khayr] to a man, and وأنْتِ بخَيْر [wa anti bi-khayr] to a woman or when you speak to more than one person.

Happy Holidays عيد مُبارك ['eed mubaarak] *(lit. a blessed celebration)* can be used for all holidays.

▎To congratulate people on their wedding, passed exams, business deals, and other successes, you can say مَبْروك [mabrook] *(lit. blessed)*. The proper response would be الله يُبارك فيك [allaah yubaarik feek] *God bless you* فيك [feek] *(sing)* or فيكُم [feekum] in the plural.

▎During Ramadan, the month of fasting in the Islamic world, you wish someone رمضان كريم [ramaDaan kareem] *(lit. a gracious Ramadan)*.

Culture Note

Islamic holidays are based on the lunar calendar and can therefore be in any of the four seasons. The most important holidays are عيد الفِطْر ['eed al-fiTr] *celebration of fast breaking* at the end of Ramadan and عيد الأضْحَى ['eed al-aDHaa] *celebration of sacrifice* which is celebrated at the time of حج [hajj] *pilgrimage* to مكّة [makkah] *Mekka*.

Useful Words

The Family العائلة 2, 4

grandfather	jadd/ajdaad	جَدّ / أجْداد	grandmother	jaddah/--aat	جَدّة / ـات
uncle (father's side)	'amm/a'maam	عَمّ / أعْمام	aunt (father's side)	'ammah/--aat	عَمّة / ـات
uncle (mother's side)	khaal/akhwaal	خال / أخْوال	aunt (mother's side)	khallah/--aat	خالة / ـات
cousin (p)	ibn 'amm	اِبْن عَمّ	f. cousin (p)	bint 'amm	بِنْت عَمّ
cousin (m)	ibn khaal	اِبْن خال	f. cousin (m)	bint khaal	بِنْت خال
nephew, from brother	ibn akh	اِبْن أخ	niece, from brother	bint akh	بِنْت أخ
nephew, from sister	ibn ukht	اِبْن أُخْت	niece, from sister	bint ukht	بِنْت أُخْت

Note: p = paternal, m = maternal

The words أب [ab] and أخ [akh] are noteworthy. When they appear in a genitive construction or with a personal suffix, a و [oo] is inserted. The exception is the personal suffix of the 1st person singular.

| my father | abee | أبي | my brother | akhee | أخي |
| Ahmad's father | aboo aHmad | أبو أحْمَد | his brother | akhoohu | أخوه |

114

 **Regional Variations**

في العامية

To Want; To Like

While Standard Arabic uses أراد — يُريد [araad -- yureed] for these verbs, Syrian Arabic uses the word بدّ [bidd] with the added personal suffix. In Egyptian Arabic, add the participle عايز ['aayiz] (sometimes عاوز) ['aawiz].

	Syrian		Egyptian	
I want; I'd like	biddee	بدّي	'aayiz (ah)	عايِز(ة)
he wants; he'd like	bidduh	بدّهُ	'aayiz	عايِز
she wants; she'd like	biddhaa	بدّها	'aayizah	عايِزة
we want; we'd like	biddnaa	بدّنا	'aayizeen	عايِزين

Regional Vocabulary

	Syrian	Egyptian
to come in	faat – bifoot	dakhal -- yidkhul
Come in!	foot(ee)	udkhul (ee)
a little present	hadeeyah Sagheerah	hadeeyah Sughayyarah
Have a seat!	u'd (ee)	u'd (ee)
to leave; to go out	Taali' -- biyTla'	kharag -- yikhrug
he told me	aallee	aallee
I want to study medicine too.	anaa kamaan biddee adrus Tibb	anaa kamaan 'aayiz adrus Tibb
I'm telling you	ba'ullak	a'ullak
Say,...!	ool (ee)	ool (ee)
milk	Haleeb	laban

115

Exercises   التمارين

1 How would you respond to these phrases? The first one has already been done for you.

1. السلام عليكم!   ..وعليكم السلام!..............
2. كيف الحال؟   ....
3. كل سنة وأنتم بخير!   ....
4. مبروك!   ....

2 Read the dialogue from this lesson again and decide which statements are true (T) or false (F).

	T	F	
1. توماس يزور عائلة أحمد في رمضان.	☒	☐
2. أحمد يعطي أمّه الحلويات.	☐	☐
3. أبو أحمد يطبخ الأكل.	☐	☐
4. أخو أحمد طبيب.	☐	☐
5. بنت أخت أحمد، اسمها نادية.	☐	☐
6. أمّ أحمد تقول «بسم الله» قبل الإفطار.	☐	☐

3 Transform Ahmad's father's statements into indirect speech as shown in the example.

1. أبو أحمد: عندي ابنين وبنت.   ..قال إنّ عنده ابنين وبنت...........
2. أبو أحمد: أحمد مهندس.   ....
3. أبو أحمد: كريم يدرس الطبّ.   ....
4. أبو أحمد: فاطمة مدرّسة.   ....
5. أبو أحمد: نحن عطشانين.   ....
6. أبو أحمد: ما شربنا منذ الصباح.   ....

4 Introduce your family using the words from the boxes.

زوج (ـة)	أب	أخ ✓	ابن	أمّ	أخت

1. هٰذا أخي..............   4. ....
2. ....   5. ....
3. ....   6. ....

5 Which words share the same root? Find the matching pairs as shown in the example.

a.	عامل	1.	درس – يدرس
b.	طبّاخ	2.	عمل – يعمل
c.	شوربة	3.	طلب – يطلب
d.	أكل	4.	طبخ – يطبخ
e.	مدرّس	5.	أرسل – يرسل
f.	طالب	6.	شرب – يشرب
g.	رسالة	7.	أكل – يأكل

6 What are the opposites?

4.	أخت	....	1.	رخيص	....
5.	أعطى – يعطي	....	2.	مستحيل	....
6.	دخل – يدخل	....	3.	شبعان	....

7 Form sentences with يريد أن *to want (to do) s.th.* as shown in the example

1. يدرس الطّب. .... يريد أن يدرس الطّب. ..
2. يذهب إلىٰ السينما. ....
3. يشتري حلويات. ....
4. يكتب رسالة. ....

8 Transform these sentences from the past tense into the present tense.

1. أرسلت إليكم رسالة. .... أرسل إليكم رسالة. ....
2. وصلت الرسالة. ....
3. أحمد أعطى أمّه الهدية. ....
4. نادية أحبّت الحلويات. ....
5. أردنا أن نذهب إلىٰ السينما. ....
6. قال لي إنّه يريد أن يدرس الطّب. ....

9 Transform these sentences from the present tense into the past tense.

1. الأصدقاء يدخلون البيت. الأصدقاء دخلوا البيت. ....
2. أمّ أحمد تطبخ الأكل. ....
3. أحمد يخرج من الغرفة. ....
4. أحمد وأبوه يرجعون. ....
5. فاطمة تضع الهدية على الطاولة. ....
6. أمّ أحمد تقول: خذوا التمر والحليب! ....

Test 2

أهلاً و سهلاً في فندق ((الشّرق))!

يقع فندقنا في قلب مدينة دمشق. كلّ غرفنا بحمام و مكيّف. في مطعمنا الجديد نقدم لكم المطبخ السوري الممتاز.

بالإضافة إلى ذلك يمكنكم أن تزوروا حديقتنا الجميلة أو محلنا للهدايا الشرقيّة. نتمنى لكم إقامة سعيدة!

1 Read the dialogue and decide which statements are true (T) or false (F).

Points ...../4

1. T ☐   F ☐

Our restaurant is located in Damascus.

2. T ☐   F ☐

Each guest room has an air conditioner and a bathroom at our hotel.

3. T ☐   F ☐

We serve Middle Eastern cuisine at our new restaurant.

4. T ☐   F ☐

At our hotel garden, we have a store that sells Middle Eastern gift items.

2 Which word doesn't fit into each category? Mark it.

☐	لون	☐	مدرّس	☐	طالب	☐	1. شرطي
☐	أحمر	☐	أسمر	☐	فواكه	☐	2. أزرق
☐	تفّاح	☐	عائلة	☐	تمر	☐	3. برتقال
☐	أمّ	☐	بلد	☐	أخ	☐	4. زوجة
☐	جُبن	☐	زُبد	☐	موز	☐	5. حليب
☐	سلطة	☐	كولا	☐	شاي	☐	6. قهوة

Points ...../6

Test 2

3 Which words shares the same root? Find the matching pairs.

a. مطبخ		1. درس
b. مدرّس		2. طبّاخ
c. مكتبة		3. كتاب
d. مقهىٰ		4. زوج
e. متزوّج		5. مفتاح
f. مفتوح		6. قهوة

Points ...../6

4 Put these sentences in the negative using: ليس، ما، لا

1. ..... أعرف إلىٰ المتحف. ....
2. ..... ذهبت إلىٰ قلب العاصمة بعد. ....
3. ..... عندي وقت. ....
4. ..... أحب القهوة مع الحليب. ....
5. ..... يوجد في البيت بهارات. ....
6. ..... اللغة العربية ..... صعبة. ....

Points ...../6

5 Complete the following sentences with the appropriate preposition.

1. أبحث .... مكتبة جيّدة.
2. أحتاج ...... قاموس عربي – إنكليزي.
3. أبو سعيد قال .... صديقي إنّ هناك مكتبة جديدة.
4. سألته .... الطريق .... هناك.
5. المكتبة مفتوحة فقط ...... الظهر. يجب أن نخرج ...... البيت الآن.
6. يمكن أن نرجع .... هنا .... المساء.

Punkte ...../6

6 Rearrange the following words to make complete sentences.

1. يدرس – أن – يريد – الطبّ – أخي.
   ....
2. أعرف – الحلويات – أنّ – يحبّون – العرب.
   ....
3. أستطيع – لا – في – أن – عيد الفطر – أزوركم.
   ....
4. الأردنّ – قرأت – جميل – أنّ – بلد.
   ....
5. هٰذه – عالية – الحمراء – الجودة – النرجيلة.
   ....
6. أنّ – إلىٰ – أذهب – أردت – السينما.
   ....

Points ...../6

English Dialogue Translations

1 Welcome!

Thomas has been learning Arabic for sometime. On the street he runs into Ahmad and Ahmad's friends Mahmood and Samirah.

Thomas:	Hi Ahmad!
Ahmad:	Hi. How are you?
Thomas:	I'm fine. How are you?
Ahmad:	Thank God, everything is ok. These are my friends. This is Mahmood, and this is Samirah.
Thomas:	Pleasure to meet you. Welcome!
Mahmood:	Hi. What's your name?
Thomas:	My name is Thomas. Where are you *(pl)* from?
Mahmood:	We are from Jordan, and Samirah is Palestinian.
Samirah:	You speak Arabic well.
Thomas:	Thank you very much.
Mahmood:	My pleasure, Thomas.
Thomas:	The pleasure is mine. Good bye.
Ahmad:	See you later, I hope. (*lit.* God willing)

2 How Much Is the Room?

Thomas is at a hotel talking to the receptionist.

Thomas:	Hello (lit. peace be with you).
hotel clerk:	Hello (lit. and peace be with you).
Thomas:	Do you have a single room?
hotel clerk:	Just a moment, please ... Yes, we have a room.
Thomas:	Do the rooms come with a bath and ... How do you say in Arabic? ... Air conditioning?
hotel clerk:	Yes, of course.
Thomas:	How much is the room?
hotel clerk:	Seven dollars per night.
Thomas:	Good. I'll take it.
hotel clerk:	For how many nights?
Thomas:	For two weeks.
hotel clerk:	May I have your passport please?
Thomas:	Excuse me? ... Oh yes, I understand. Here's my passport.
hotel clerk:	. ... Welcome to our hotel! Here, ... this is your key.
Thomas:	Thank you.
hotel clerk:	You're welcome.

3 New in Town

Thomas is asking two people for directions to the National Museum.

Thomas:	Excuse me, ma'am. Where is the National Museum? Is it far?
woman:	No, it's nearby. Go this way to Palestine Street. Then, straight ahead to New Square. And from there make a left, and After about 50 meters you'll see an old building on the right. The museum is next to this building.
Thomas:	Thank you very much. Good bye.
woman:	Good bye. (*lit.* God will protect you.)
Shortly afterwards) ...	
Thomas:	Excuse me, do you know how to get to National Museum?
man:	Sure. Follow me!
Thomas:	Many thanks. I'm new in town. I've been here for three days.
man:	How about a little tour through the old town?
Thomas:	That would be great!

English Dialogue Translations

To the Center of Town

Thomas is standing on the sidewalk flagging down a taxi. The taxi stops and Thomas gets in.

Thomas:	Good morning.
taxi driver:	Good morning, sir.
Thomas:	To the town center, please.
taxi driver:	Certainly, sir.
Thomas:	And do you have a meter?
taxi driver:	Of course. Here's the meter … Your Arabic is great!
Thomas:	But Arabic is not easy.
taxi driver:	Have you been to an Arabic-speaking country before?
Thomas:	Yes, I was in Morocco two years ago, and three years ago in the United Arab Emirates.
taxi driver:	What do you think of the capital of our beautiful country?
Thomas:	It's very pretty and the people are good-natured and friendly.
taxi driver:	Here we are, sir. This is the center of town.
Thomas:	Great. Could you please stop on the right. How much?
taxi driver:	Pay what you'd like.

On the Phone

Samirah talks to her friend Fatima.

Samirah:	Hello!
Faatimah:	Hello Samirah. How are you?
Samirah:	I'm fine, thanks. Who's this?
Faatimah:	It's me, Faatimah.
Samirah:	Hi Faatimah, how are you?
Faatimah:	Everything is OK. I called you yesterday. Where were you? What were you doing?
Samirah:	In the morning I was in the office and I wrote some letters. In the afternoon I bought some things at the market. And in the evening I went with my friends to the movies.
Faatimah:	Do you have any free time today?
Samirah:	What time is it?
Faatimah:	One o'clock.
Samirah:	I'm sorry but I have an appointment at 2:30, but I do have time tomorrow.
Faatimah:	Excellent! Stop by our house in the evening.
Samirah:	That would be great. At what time?
Faatimah:	At 8:00.
Samirah:	Great. See you tomorrow, I hope. (*lit.* God willing.)

6 Abu Saied's Coffee Shop

Ahmad and Thomas go to a coffee shop and sit down at one of the tables.

Ahmad:	This is Abu Saied's coffee shop. Abu Saied is very nice. You'll see.
Abu Saied:	Good evening, guys.
Ahmad:	Good evening, Abu Saeid. How are you? How's the family?
Abu Saied:	Thank God, everything is fine. What are you having?
Ahmad:	Tea, please.
Abu Saied:	Right away… Who's this?
Ahmad:	This is my friend Thomas. He's studying Arabic and he'll be working here at the hospital.
Abu Saied:	Welcome. My name is Abu Saeid. Do you understand Arabic?
Thomas:	I speak a little Arabic.
Abu Saied:	Are you married?
Thomas:	Yes, my wife is an engineer at an international company.

122

English Dialogue Translations

Abu Saied:	And, what do you do?
Thomas:	I'm a doctor.
Abu Saied:	Do you have any children?
Thomas:	Yes, I have a son and a daughter.
Abu Saied:	How old are they?
Thomas:	My son is six years old and my daughter is four years old.
Abu Saied:	That's nice. (*lit.* What God wants.)

7 At the Souk

Ahmad is looking for a present and talks to a vendor at the souk.

merchant:	Hello, sir. What can I do for you?
Ahmad:	Hi. I need a present. I'm looking for something Middle Eastern.
merchant:	Welcome. I have everything, hookah, gold, silver, fabrics ...
Ahmad:	Can I see the hookah (water pipe)?
merchant:	Of course. I have many colors and shapes. Would you like some tea?
Ahmad:	Yes with very little sugar, please.
merchant:	Here you are. Have a seat over here, sir.
Ahmad:	How much is this big yellow hookah?
merchant:	It's a bargain. Only 900 pounds.
Ahmad:	That's too expensive. I can only pay you 600 pounds.
merchant:	No, that's really impossible. This is a high quality hookah. Why don't you get a small one. This red hookah is cheaper. It is only 800 pounds.
Ahmad:	And the blue one over there. How much is it?
merchant:	I'll give you a good price. 750 pounds.
Ahmad:	I only have 700 pounds.
merchant:	Your not making this easy. OK, OK, the hookah is 700 pounds.
Ahmad:	Good, I'll take the blue hookah.
merchant:	Congratulations (*lit.* may you be blessed), sir. That's really a nice present.
Ahmad:	Thank you. (*lit.* God bless you.)

Note: *A hookah is a waterpipe used for smoking tabacco and herbal fruits. It is also called a sisha, waterpipe or nargile.*

8 At the Restaurant

Mahmood and Samirah are sitting in a restaurant waiting for Ahmad who seems to be running late.

Samirah:	I'm hungry. Should we order or wait for Ahmad?
Mahmood:	Let's wait for him a little longer.
Ahmad:	Good evening, guys... Sorry I'm late. Did you order?
Samirah:	No, we've been waiting for you. What should we have?
Ahmad:	I don't know. What do want?
Mahmood:	I'd like a salad, lentil soup and chicken with rice.
Samirah:	That's a good idea. But I don't like lentils. I prefer vegetable soup.
Mahmood:	Waiter (*lit.* sir)!
waiter:	Good evening. Are you ready to order?
Mahmood:	Yes, we 'll have salad, vegetable soup and chicken with rice.
waiter:	Anything to drink? We have cola, fruit juice...
Mahmood:	Cola, please.
waiter:	Here you go. Enjoy your meal.
Samirah:	Excuse me, we didn't order lentil soup, we ordered vegetable soup.
waiter:	I'm sorry. I'll bring it right away.
Mahmood:	Waiter (*lit.* brother), the check please.
Ahmad:	No, no. my treat.
Mahmood:	No, way that 's out of the question! (This one is on me.)

English Dialogue Translations

9) Have a Blessed Ramadam!

Thomas is visiting Ahmad's family during Ramadan.

Thomas:	Hello (*lit.* peace be with you)! Have a blessed Ramadan.
Ahmad:	Hello (*lit.* and peace with you)! Please, come in. How are you?
Thomas:	I'm fine, thank God. Here, a little present, sweets for the family.
Ahmad:	Thank you very much.
Ahmad:	Have a seat, Thomas. This is my brother Kareem. I'll give the sweets to my mother. She's in the kitchen cooking with my sister.
Kareem:	My brother told me that you are a doctor. I'd like to study medicine too.
Thomas:	That's a great idea. Hospitals need good doctors.
Ahmad:	Thomas, this is my father. Dad, this is my friend Thomas.
Abu Ahmad:	Welcome. Welcome to our home. Are you hungry?
Thomas:	No, I'm full. But you've been fasting since this morning.
Abu Ahmad:	We are not very hungry. But let me tell you, we are thirsty.
Ahmad:	This is my mother, and this is my sister Faatimah. And this is Nadja, her daughter. She's three years old. Come here, Nadja. Say hi to uncle Thomas.
Umm Ahmad:	In the name of God, let's eat (*lit.* breaking the fast). Here, Thomas, have some dates and some milk.
Ahmad:	Enjoy your meal.

Listening and Speaking

Listening and Speaking

This is the Listening and Speaking section of your book. Before we begin, here are a few tips about working with the exercises: Before you start the audio CD first refer to the instruction lines in your book, then listen to the instructions on the CD. In most repetition exercises you will hear words or expressions twice which you should then repeat twice. We also provide pauses for you to think about your answers to the given tasks. Finally, texts or dialogues are often repeated at the end of an exercise to make sure that you have understood what you have heard.

Pre-Lesson

1 In order for you to get used to the sounds of the Arabic language, listen to the pronunciation of the Arabic letters and the example words as they appear in your book. Try to read along in your book. Repeat each letter and the example twice after the speaker.

2 Listen and repeat each word along with the article twice.

دجاج ← الدّجاج

3 Listen and repeat the numbers from 0 to 10 twice.

4 Listen these three telephone phone numbers. Repeat each digit twice, then check the box with the correct telephone number in your book.

	First Number			Second Number			Third Number	
1. a.	03 72 21	☐	2. a.	46 44 67	☐	3. a.	08 75 65	☐
b.	03 22 17	☐	b.	41 64 55	☐	b.	08 09 63	☐
c.	03 77 22	☐	c.	41 64 78	☐	c.	08 99 63	☐

5 Arabic is spoken in many countries. There are three major regions in the Arabic speaking world: the West, the East, and the Arabic Peninsula which includes the Gulf region. Listen to the names of the Arabic speaking countries as they appear in the Pre-Lesson in your book. Try to read along and repeat each country twice after the speaker.

125

Listening and Speaking

Lesson 1   الدرس الأول

1 This exercise is about the pronunciation of the letter [h]. There is no real equivalent in English but you might recognize the sound from words like house or hear. Listen to each word and repeat it twice.

2 The pronunciation of the letter [ch] is a little stronger than [h]. Listen to each word with the [ch] sound and repeat it twice.

3 Now you'll hear some important expressions. Repeat them twice and pay special attention to the [h] and [ch] sounds.

4 You'll hear three short conversations in which people state their names. Repeat each name twice, then check the box with the names that were mentioned.

1. a.	Kareem	☐	2. a.	Hameed	☐	3. a.	Samirah	☐
b.	Sameer	☐	b.	Mahmood	☐	b.	Faatimah	☐
c.	Ahmad	☐	c.	Muhammad	☐	c.	Kareemah	☐

5 This exercise is about personal pronouns. After you've listened to a sentence, replace the name with the appropriate pronoun in the pause that we provide for you. You'll then hear the correct sentence. After you've heard the correct sentence repeat it twice.

من أين أحمد؟   ←   من أين هو؟

6 This exercise is about nationalities and their corresponding adjective forms. You'll hear several sentences with the names of certain countries. Change the sentences by using the adjective form for each country.

انا من ألمانيا.   ←   انا ألماني.

7 Martin is talking to someone. First listen to the dialogue. Then take Martin's role.
Respond appropriately to what was said by following the instructions.
Return the greeting.
Say that you're fine and ask how <u>she</u> is.
Say what your name is.
Say the *pleasure is mine too*.

Lesson 2   الدرس الثاني

1 This exercise is about the pronunciation of the letter [q]. It sounds a little like the English letter [k] but coming from the back of your throat. Listen to each word and repeat it twice.

2 The letter [khaaʾ] stands for a sound that is formed in the back of your throat. Listen to the words with the [khaaʾ] sound and repeat them twice.

3 In this exercise you'll hear several short sentences with proper responses that you can use in general conversations. Repeat them twice and pay special attention to the [q] and [khaaʾ] sounds.

4 Since there are no predictable rules, the plural form of each Arabic noun has to be memorized. In your book, these plural forms are listed next to the singular forms. In this vocabulary exercise you'll hear the singular form of a noun first. Try to say the plural form in the pause provided. Then you'll hear the correct plural form. Repeat it twice in the pauses provided.

مدينة   ←   مدن

Listening and Speaking

5 You'll hear two short conversations that take place in the reception area of a hotel. Listen closely to the conversations. In your book mark; how long the woman and the man want to stay in the hotel and how much the room costs. Make notes while you're listening.

2. السيّد   1. السيّدة

....   a. كم ليلة؟

....   b. بكم الغرفة؟

Lesson 3   الدرس الثالث

1 a. In this exercise you will hear word pairs that sound similar. Listen to words and repeat them twice.

b. Now you'll hear only one of the words from the word pairs of Exercise 1a. Listen to each word and repeat it twice. Then mark it in your book.

☐	عشرين	☐	عشرة	6.	☐	هناك	☐	هنا	1.
☐	تسعين	☐	سبعين	7.	☐	حال	☐	هل	2.
☐	صغير	☐	سرير	8.	☐	مفتاح	☐	متحف	3.
☐	جامع	☐	شارع	9.	☐	على	☐	الله	4.
☐	أمام	☐	أيّام	10.	☐	بعيد	☐	بعد	5.

2 This vocabulary exercise is about plural forms again. Listen to the singular form and add the plural form as you hear it in the example.

محطّة   ←   محطّات

3 You'll hear a series of numbers. Listen and repeat each number twice. Then mark it in the box in your book.

10	73	21	85	45
30	11	32	56	33
69	31	12	98	20
29	57	97	13	34
68	86	22	74	44

4 This exercise is about combining numbers with nouns. First you'll hear a number. In the pause provided, create combinations—number with day [youm] / days [ayahm] and night [lehlah] / nights [lehyahlee].

أربعة   ←   أربعة أيّام وأربع ليالي

127

Listening and Speaking

5 In this exercise you will practice how to use adjectives. First you'll hear a noun in the singular or plural form. In the pauses provided add to each noun the adjectives *big* [kahbeer] and *small* [sahreer].

المحطّة   →   المحطّة الكبيرة والمحطّة الصغيرة

6 In this short conversation a woman is asking for directions. Where does she want to go? Listen and mark the correct answer in your book.

c. إلى البنايات الجديدة ☐   a. إلى الساحة الجديدة ☐

d. إلى السوق القديمة ☐   b. إلى الشارع الكبير ☐

Lesson 4 / الدرس الرابع

1 This vocabulary exercise is about plural forms. Listen to the singular form and add the plural form as you hear it in the example. After you've heard the correct form, repeat it twice in the pauses provided.

مطعم   →   مطاعم

2 This exercise is about genitive combinations. First you'll hear a genitive without the article. In the pause, say the genitive constructions along <u>with</u> the article. After you've heard the correct form, repeat it twice. Note that the main word itself doesn't have an article.

سائق تاكسي   →   سائق التاكسي

3 Imagine you are sitting in a taxi. Tell the driver where you want to go following the example.

مركز المدينة   →   إلى مركز المدينة ، من فضلك.

4 Now practice the conjugation of the verb [kahn]. Change the sentences into the first person singular in the pauses that are provided for you. After you've heard the correct phrase, repeat it twice.

كنّا في المغرب قبل ثلاث سنوات.   →   كنت في المغرب قبل ثلاث سنوات.

Listening and Speaking

Lesson 5 — الدرس الخامس

1 a. Listen to these similar sounding word pairs and repeat them twice in the pauses.

b. Listen to these words and repeat them twice. Then mark them in your book.

☐	دقائق	☐	أصدقاء	6.	☐	مطار	☐	قطار	1.
☐	نصف	☐	ناس	7.	☐	ساعة	☐	ساحة	2.
☐	الأربعاء	☐	أربعة	8.	☐	كثير	☐	كبير	3.
☐	ليلة	☐	ليلاً	9.	☐	اليمن	☐	اليمين	4.
☐	مساءً	☐	مساء	10.	☐	شاي	☐	شيء	5.

2 This vocabulary exercise is about plural forms. Listen to the singular form and add the plural form as you hear it in the example. After you've heard the correct form, repeat it twice in the pauses provided.

رسالة ← رسائل

3 This exercise is about telling time. Answer the questions about the time of the day following the instructions. After you hear the correct time, repeat it twice.

4 You'll hear a conversation between Sameer and Kareemah. Listen closely and make notes about where they were yesterday morning, yesterday afternoon and yesterday evening. Then mark your findings in your book.

2. كريمة   1. سامر

a. في الصباح   ....

b. بعد الظهر   ....

Listening and Speaking

Lesson 6 / الدرس السادس

1 Listen to these professions, then say their feminine forms in the pauses provided. After you hear the correct feminine forms, repeat them twice.

مخرج → مخرجة

2 This exercise is about present tense verb forms. In the pauses that are provided for you, change the past tense sentences you hear into the present tense. After you've heard the correct present tense form, repeat it twice.

درس في الجامعة. → يدرس في الجامعة.

3 Listen to these statements and respond appropriately in the pauses provided. After you've heard the responses, repeat them twice.

4 You're having a conversation with a woman. Follow the instructions below as you to speak to her.
Ask her what her profession is.
Ask her if she's married.
Ask her if she has children.
Ask her how old they are.

Lesson 7 / الدرس السابع

1 a. Listen to these similar sounding word pairs and repeat them twice.

b. Listen to these words and repeat them twice. Then mark them in your book.

☐	سأل	☐	صعب	6.	☐	أحمر	☐	1. أحمد
☐	شكل	☐	شكر	7.	☐	حال	☐	2. محلّ
☐	جولة	☐	جودة	8.	☐	عالي	☐	3. على
☐	طيّب	☐	طبيب	9.	☐	ما	☐	4. مع
☐	جدّاً	☐	جيّد	10.	☐	تسعمائة	☐	5. سبعمائة

2 Now you'll hear sentences with singular nouns. Say these sentences replacing the singular form with the plural forms in the pauses provided. After you've heard the correct form, repeat it twice.

يشتغل في شركة. → يشتغل في شركات.

3 Create the imperative or command forms as you hear it in the example. After you've heard the correct forms repeat them twice.

إذهبوا إلى المحلّ! → اذهبون إلى المحلّ.

Listening and Speaking

4 You'll hear a conversation in a store. Two men are haggling about the price of a water pipe. Listen closely and make notes about the the prices you hear. Then write them in Arabic in your book in the order you hear them.

1. ... ٣٠٠ ...   5. ....
2. ....   6. ....
3. ....   7. ....
4. ....   8. ....

الدرس الثامن — Lesson 8

1 This exercise is about the plural forms again. Listen to the singular form and add the plural form as you hear it in the example. After you've heard the correct form, repeat it twice in the pauses provided.

محلّ   ←   محلّات

2 You are at a market asking for the prices of various food items. Listen to the answers and write the prices per kilogram كيلو onto the lines in your book.

الليمون   ←   لو سمحت ، بكم الليمون؟

131

Listening and Speaking

3 This exercise is about negative forms in the present tense. Listen to the sentences and change them into negative sentences. After you've heard the negative sentence repeat them twice.

نأكل في هذا المطعم. ← لا نأكل في هذا المطعم.

4 You'll hear three short dialogues that take place in a restaurant. In each dialogue, a guest is ordering from the menu. While listening, make notes and mark in your book which orders match which dialogue.

1. Dialogue 1   a. السلطة والدجاج مع الرزّ
2. Dialogue 2   b. شوربة الخضر ولحم الغنم مع البطاطا
3. Dialogue 3   c. شوربة العدس والكباب

Lesson 9 — الدرس التاسع

1 Listen to each word and repeat it twice. Pay special attention to the differences between HJRAH and HA.

2 Listen and respond appropriately. After you've heard the response, repeat it twice.

3 Samirah is showing you a family photo album. Listen and mark in your book which statements are true (T) or false (F). The first one has already been done for you.

	T	F	
1.	☒	☐	أخوها الكبير اسمه طارق.
2.	☐	☐	أختها مهندسة.
3.	☐	☐	أخوها كريم يدرس الطبّ.
4.	☐	☐	كريم متزوّج.

4 Listen to these statements and change them into indirect speech. After you've heard the correct sentence, repeat it twice.

ذهبت إلى السوق. ← قال إنّه ذهب إلى السوق.

Answer Key: Lessons

Pre-Lesson

1. 1. d — 2. c — 3. f — 4. e — 5. b — 6. a
2. 1. 2007 — 2. 1999 — 3. 1963 — 4. 1985 — 5. 1951 — 6. 1643
3. 1. السعودية — 3. السودان — 4. النور — 6. الشمس
4. 1. الدرس — 2. البيت — 3. الخبز — 4. الأخبار — 5. الصباح — 6. السلام
5. 1. باب — 2. سلام — 3. واحد — 4. صباح — 5. ألمانيا — 6. الإمارات
6. 1. ا ا — 2. د — 3. ذ — 4. ر — 5. ز — 6. و
7. 1. شُكْراً — 2. إِلـىٰ — 3. جَـوْلَـة — 4. أَهْـلاً — 5. لُـغَـة — 6. أُحِـبّ

Lesson 1

الدرس الأول

1. 1. — 2. — 4. — 5.
2. 1. d — 2. f — 3. e — 4. a — 5. c — 6. b
3. 1. هو مصري. هي مصرية. — 2. هو سوري. هي سورية. — 3. هو ألماني. هي ألمانية. — 4. هو أردنّي. هي أردنّية. — 5. هو فلسطيني. هي فلسطينية.
4. 1. أنا — 2. هم — 3. هو — 4. هي — 5. أنت
5. *(In order to avoid confusion in the non-vocalized script, try to write the vowels in English with the appropriate letter.)*
6. 1. أنا بخير — 2. اسمي... — 3. أنا من ألمانيا — 4. لا، أنا ألماني (ــة)
7. 1. أهلاً يا أحمد! — 2. كيف الحال؟ — 3. هؤلاء — 4. هذا — 5. هذا — 6. هذه

133

Answer Key: Lessons

Lesson 2
الدرس الثاني

1 1. لا — 2. نعم — 3. نعم

2 1. b — 2. c — 3. d — 4. a

3 1. مساء الخير! — 2. عندكم غرفة بسرير واحد؟ — 3. ليلتين. — 4. بكم الغرفة؟

4

	مدينة		جواز	
	Plural	Singular	Plural	Singular
1. Person	مدينتنا	مدينتي	جوازنا	جوازي
2. Person	مدينتكم	مدينتَك	جوازكم	جوازَك
		مدينتِك		جوازِك
3. Person	مدينتهم	مدينته	جوازهم	جوازه
		مدينتها		جوازها

5 1. مدينتين — 2. طفلين — 3. موظّفين — 4. غرفتين — 5. سريرين — 6. أسبوعين

6 1. c — 2. b — 3. a

7 1. مدينة — 2. جواز — 3. ليلة — 4. أسبوع — 5. ألماني — 6. مفتاح

8 1. أردنيّين — 2. بيوت — 3. طاولات — 4. غرف — 5. أطفال — 6. سوريات

9 1. عندي طفلين. — 2. عنده جوازين. — 3. عندنا فندق. — 4. عندكم غرفة بسريرين؟ — 5. عندك المفتاح؟ — 6. عندها حديقة.

10 [shoo ismuh bi-l-'arabee?]

11 [ismaha eh?]

Lesson 3
الدرس الثالث

1 a. أين المدينة القديمة؟ — b. أين الساحة الجديدة؟ — c. أين الجامع الكبير؟

2 إلى المحطة

3 1. d — 2. b — 3. a — 4. e — 5. c

4 1. أيّام — 2. بناية — 3. ليلة — 4. أمتار — 5. جوامع — 6. طريق

Answer Key: Lessons

5 1. — the big mosque 2. — a new day 3. — The markets are old.
   4. — My house is nearby.

6 1. غرفة صغيرة — 2. جواز سوري — 3. محطّة كبيرة — 4. مطعم عربي

7 1. الشارع الكبير — 2. البيت العربي — 3. البناية الجديدة — 4. الطفل الصغير

8 1. مدن جديدة — 2. الحدائق الصغيرة — 3. الساحات القديمة — 4. طاولات كبيرة

9 1. هو بعيد. — 2. هي كبيرة. — 3. هي قديمة. — 4. هم عرب.

10 1. في — 2. جنب — 3. أمام — 4. فوق ، على

الدرس الرابع

Lesson 4

1 في البيت: غرفة ، باب ، طاولة ، مطبخ — في المدينة: ساحة ، شارع ، سيّارة ، باص

2 1. b. — 2. d. — 3. c. — 4. a. — 5. f. — 6. e.

3 باب المكتبة ، باب السيّارة ، مفتاح الباب ، مفتاح الجامعة ، مفتاح الباص ، سائق السيّارة ، سائق الباص ، مكتبة الجامعة ، مكتبة الأطفال ...

4 1. غرفة النوم الصغيرة — 2. مركز المدينة القديم — 3. بناية مدرسة كبيرة — 4. سائقي تاكسي لطفاء

5 مفاعل: مراكز ، مدارس ، مطاعم ، متاحف — ــات: مطارات ، مكتبات ، سينمات ، محطّات

6 1. لست إنكليزي. — 2. لسنا من ألمانيا. — 3. الجامعة ليست قريبة. — 4. السوق ليست كبيرة.

7 1. المدينة كانت كبيرة. — 2. العاصمة كانت جميلة. — 3. كنّا في بلد عربي. — 4. الناس كانوا طيّبين ولطفاء.

8 1. منذ — 2. من قبل — 3. قبل — 4. قبل

9 1. نعم ، كان في بلد عربي من قبل. — 2. كان في المغرب و في الإمارات.

10 1. a. المدرسة مش بعيدة. b. المدرسة مو بعيدة. — 2. a. هو مش من مصر. b. هو مو من مصر.

الدرس الخامس

Lesson 5

1 1. فعلت — 2. كنت — 3. شربت — 4. ذهبت — 5. اشتريت

2 1. كانت في المكتب وكتبت رسائل. — 2. اشترَت أشياء من السوق. — 3. ذهبَت مع أصدقائها إلى السينما.

3 1. ظهراً — 2. بعد الظهر — 3. مساءً — 4. ليلاً — 5. صباحاً

4 1. الساعة احدى عشر — 2. الساعة ثلاثة وعشر دقائق — 3. الساعة خمسة وثلث — 4. الساعة ستة ونصف — 5. الساعة عشرة إلاّ ربع

5 1. — 3. — 5. نعم ، عندي وقت. — 2. — 4. — 6. أنا آسف (ــة) ، عندي موعد.

135

Answer Key: Lessons

6 1. راحوا إلى السينما. – 2. راحوا إلى السوق. – 3. راحوا إلى الجامعة.

7 1. ماذا فعلت أمس؟ – 2. ['amalt eh imbaariH]

8 1. عندك وقت اليوم؟ – 2. غداً ، إن شاء الله.

Lesson 6 الدرس السادس

1 1. T – 2. T – 3. T – 4. T – 5. T

2 1. ذهبوا إلى المقهى. – 2. شربوا شاي. – 3. نعم ، توماس متزوّج. – 4. تشتغل زوجته كمهندسة. – 5. عمره ستّ سنوات. – 6. عمرها أربع سنوات.

3 1. يشتغل الطبيب في المستشفى. – 2. يشتغل التاجر في السوق. – 3. تشتغل الراقصة في المسرح. – 4. يشتغل المدرّس في المدرسة. – 5. يشتغل السائق في السيّارة. – 6. يشتغل الطبّاخ في المطبخ.

4 1. موظّفة – 2. مترجمة – 3. صيدلية – 4. مهندسة – 5. طالبة – 6. حلاّقة

5 1. يذهب إلى الجامعة. – 2. يشربون قهوة. – 3. تعرفين كثيراً. – 4. أرى / ترى الأهرام في مصر – 5. تسكن العائلة في دمشق. – 6. ندرس اللّغة العربية.

6 1. سيتكلّمون اللغة الألمانية. – 2. سيشتغل في شركة. – 3. ستفهم العربية. – 4. أين سنجلس؟ – 5. ماذا سيفعل؟ – 6. ستسكنون في الفندق.

7 استعمال اللغة (Compare your answers with the variations under "Talking about Family and Profession" in column:

Lesson 7 الدرس السابع

1 1. لو سمحت ، أبحث عن طاولة. – 2. تفضّل ، عندي طاولات كثيرة. – 3. بكم هذه؟ – 4. بستّمائة ليرة. – 5. طيّب ، آخذ الطاولة. – 6. مبروك! – 7. الله يبارك فيك!

2 1. أحتاج إلى هدية. – 2. أبحث عن محلّ. – 3. أسأل عن الأسعار.

3 1. بتسعمائة ليرة. – 2. بثمانمائة ليرة. – 3. بسبعمائة وخمسين ليرة. – 4. يدفع سبعمائة ليرة.

4 1. إذهب إلى اليسار! – 2. إذهبي إلى اليسار! – 3. إجلس هنا! – 4. إجلسي هنا! – 5. إشرب الشاي! – 6. إشربي الشاي!

5 1. إعمل لي سعر جيّد! – 2. إسأل عن أبو سعيد! – 3. خذ الحزام الأسود! – 4. إجلسي جنب الشبّاك! – 5. أكتبي رسالة!

6 1. g. – 2. f. – 3. a. – 4. c. – 5. d. – 6. e. – 7. b.

7 1. نحتاج إليه. – 2. المفتاح عليها. – 3. تبحثون عنه. – 4. كنت عندهم. – 5. يسأل عنه. – 6. ذهب إليها.

136

Answer Key: Lessons

الدرس الثامن

Lesson 8

1 1. بقدونس – 3. بصل – 4. خيار – 5. طماطم – 8. ليمون – 9. نعناع

2 1. ماء – 2. فواكه – 3. خبز – 4. بيض

3 1. انتظره. – 2. أكلها. – 3. درسها. – 4. سألها.

4 1. أشرب كأس ماء. – 2. أكتب رسائل. – 3. أشتري فواكه. – 4. أدفع الحساب.

5 1. أخذت السمك والرزّ. – 2. عرفت الطريق إلى المتحف. – 3. سكنت في بلد عربي. – 4. فهمت الإنكليزية؟

6 1. لا أحبّ الشوربة ، أفضّل السلطة. – 2. لا أحبّ القهوة ، أفضّل الشاي. – 3. لا أحبّ الكولا ، أفضّل العصير. – 4. لا أحبّ التفّاح ، أفضّل البرتقال.

7 1. ما – 2. ما – 3. لا – 4. لا

8 1. يا سيدي! – 2. نأخذ لحم الغنم مع البطاطا. – 3. لو سمحت ، ما طلبنا الرزّ، طلبنا البطاطا. – 4. الحساب ، من فضلك.

الدرس التاسع

Lesson 9

1 1. وعليكم السلام! – 2. أنا بخير ، الحمد لله. – 3. وأنت / أنتم بخير! – 4. الله يبارك فيك / فيكم!

2 1. T – 2. T – 3. F – 4. F – 5. T – 6. T

3 1. قال إنّ عنده ابنين وبنت. – 2. قال إنّ أحمد مهندس. – 3. قال إنّ كريم يدرس الطبّ. – 4. قال إنّ فاطمة مدرّسة. – 5. قال إنّهم عطشانين. – 6. قال إنّهم ما شربوا منذ الصباح.

4 1. هذا أخي. – 2. هذا زوجي. / هذه زوجتي. – 3. هذا أبي. – 4. هذا ابني. – 5. هذه أمّي. – 6. هذه أختي.

5 1. e. – 2. a. – 3. f. – 4. b. – 5. g. – 6. c. – 7. d.

6 1. غالي – 2. ممكن – 3. جوعان – 4. أخ – 5. أخذ – يأخذ – 6. خرج – يخرج

7 1. يريد أن يدرس الطبّ. – 2. يريد أن يذهب إلى السينما. – 3. يريد أن يشتري حلويات. – 4. يريد أن يكتب رسالة.

8 1. أرسل إليكم رسالة. – 2. تصل الرسالة. – 3. أحمد يعطي أمّه الحلويات. – 4. نادية تحبّ الحلويات. – 5. نريد أن نذهب إلى السينما. – 6. يقول لي إنّه يريد أن يدرس الطبّ.

9 1. الأصدقاء دخلوا البيت. – 2. أمّ أحمد طبخت الأكل. – 3. أحمد خرج من الغرفة. – 4. أحمد وأبوه رجعوا. – 5. فاطمة وضعت الهدية على الطاولة. – 6. أمّ أحمد قالت: خذوا التمر والحليب

137

Answer Key: Tests

34–26 points: مُمْتاز! – Great job!

25–17 points: جيّد! – You made good progress point.

less than 17 points: العربيّة لَيْسَت سهْلة. – You can improve! Review grammar and vocabulary sections of the last 5 lessons again.

Test 1

1. 1. F — 2. F — 3. F — 4. T

2. 1. هنا — 2. قديم — 3. بعيد — 4. تحت — 5. قبل — 6. كبير

3. 1. سيّد — 2. بلد — 3. صديق — 4. مفتاح — 5. قهوة — 6. جواز

4. 1. متاحف — 2. مطاعم — 3. مطابخ — 4. مراكز — 5. مكاتب — 6. مدارس

5. 1. فندق قديم — 2. سيّارات جديدة — 3. أطفال صغار — 4. أشياء كثيرة — 5. موظّفة لطيفة — 6. سيّدات جميلات

6. 1. e — 2. d — 3. f — 4. a — 5. c — 6. b

Test 2

1. 1. F — 2. T — 3. F — 4. F

2. 1. لون — 2. فواكه — 3. عائلة — 4. بلد — 5. موز — 6. سلطة

3. 1. b — 2. a — 3. c — 4. e — 5. f — 6. d

4.
1. لا
2. ما
3. ما or ليس
4. لا
5. لا
6. ليست

5. 1. عن — 2. إلىٰ — 3. لـِ — 4. عن ، إلىٰ — 5. حتىٰ ، من — 6. إلىٰ ، في

6. 1. أخي يريد أن يدرس الطبّ. — 2. أعرف أنّ العرب يحبّون الحلويات. — 3. لا أستطيع أن أزوركم في عيد الفطر. — 4. قرأت أنّ الأردنّ بلد جميل. — 5. هٰذه النرجبلة الحصاء عالية الجودة. — 6. أردت أنْ أذهب إلىٰ السينما.

Glossary

ut, حَوالَي, [Hawalee], 3
or (m), مُمَثِّل / ـين, [muththil/--een], 6
er (time), بَعْد, [ba'd], 3
er that, بَعْد ذلِك, [ba'd thaalik], 3
, قَبْل, [qabl], 4
conditioning, مُكَيِّف, [mukayyif], 2
port, مَطار / ـات, [maTaar/--at], 4
eria, الجَزائِر, [al-jazaa'ir], Pre-Lesson
the best!, كُلّ سَنة وَأنتُم بِخَيْر, [kull sanah wa antum bi-khayr], 9
ow me, لَوْ سَمَحْت, [law samaHt], 7
o, أيضاً, [ayDan], 2
herican (f), أمريكِيّة, [amreekeeyah], 1
herican (m), أمريكي, [amreekee], 1
d, وَ, [wa], 1
pointment, مَوعِد / مَواعيد, [maw'id / mawaa'eed], 5
abic (m), عَرَبي, ['arabee], 1
abic; the Arabic language, العَرَبيّة, [al-'arabeeyah], 4
a, مِنْطَقة, [minTaqah], 4
, كَـ, [ka], 6
much as you like. (lit. Suit yourself.), كَما تُريد, [kamaa tureed], 4
de, جانِباً, [jaaniban], 8
k!, إسْألوا, [is'aloo], 7
what time? (lit. to which hour?),?في أيّ ساعة, [fee ayy saa'ah], 5
with; to have, عِنْد, ['ind], 2
hrain, البَحْرَين, [al-baHrayn], Pre-Lesson
th (room), حَمّام / ـات, [Hammaam/--aat], 2
autiful, pretty, nice, جَميل / ـين, [jameel/--een], 4
d, سَرير / أسِرّة, [sareer/asirrah], 2
fore; already, مِن قَبْل, [min qabl], 4
lt, حِزام / أحْزِمة, [Hizaam/'aHzimah], 4
st, أحْسَن, [aHsan], 9
st; dearest, TK, [aTyab], 9
l, حِساب / ـات, [Hisaab/--aat], 8
ack pepper, فِلْفِل أسْوَد, [filfil aswad], 8
essed, مُبارَك, [mubaarak], 9
ue, (f) زَرْقاء, [zarqaa'], 7
y; son, (pl:) children, وَلَد / أوْلاد, [wald/awlaad], 6
ass, نُحاس, [nuHaas], 7
eaking the fast; breakfast, إفْطار, [ifTaar], 9
other, أخ / إخْوة, [akh/ikhwah], 9
other! (address for a stranger), !يا أخ, [yaa akh], 8
ilding, بِناية / ـات, [binaayah/--aat], 3
lgur, بُرْغُل, [burghul], 8
nch, حِزْمة, [Hizmah], 8
s, باص / ـات, [baaS/--aat], 4
t, لكِن, [laakin], 4
airo, القاهِرة, [al-qaahirah], 1

capital, عاصِمة / عَواصِم, ['aaSimah/'awaaSim], 4
car, سَيّارة / ـات, [sayyaarah/--aat], 4
center, مَرْكَز / مَراكِز, [markaz/maraakiz], 4
certainly, عَلى عَيْني, ['alaa 'aynee], 4
charge, أُجْرة, ['ujrah], 4
cheap, رَخيص, [rakheeS], 7
chicken, دَجاج, [dajaaj], 8
child, طِفْل / أطْفال, [Tifl /aTfaal], 2
clerk; staff, مُوَظَّف / ـين, [muwaTHaf/--een], 2
coffee, قَهوة, [qahwah], 5
cola, كولا, [koolaa], 8
color, لَوْن / ألوان, [lawn/alwaan], 7
Come (f) here!, تَعالي, [ta'aalee], 9
come!, تَعالى, [ta'aalaa], 5
Come! (m), تَعال, [ta'aal], 3
Comoros, جُزُر القُمُر, [juzur al-qumur], Pre-Lesson
company, شَرِكة / ـات, [sharikah/--aat], 6
condition, حال / أحْوال, [Haal/aHwaal], 6
congratulations!, مَبْروك, [mabrook], 7
country, بَلَد / بُلْدان, [balad/buldaan], 4
cucumbers, خِيار, [khiyaar], 8
dad, بابا, [baabaa], 9
Dahab (ocean resort on Sinai), دَهَب, [dahab], 2
Damascus, دِمَشْق, [dimashq], 1
dancer (f), راقِصة, [raaqiSah], 6
date of birth, تاريخ الميلاد, [taareekh al-meelaad], 1
dates, تَمْر, [tamr], 9
day, يَوْم / أيّام, [yawm/ayyaam], 3
dear, عَزيز / أعِزّاء, ['azeez/a'izzaa'], 9
decoration, زينة, [zeenah], 8
delay, تأْخير, [ta'kheer], 8
difficult/hard, صَعْب / ـين, [Sa'b/--een], 7
dinner, عَشاء, ['ashaa'], 8
(slang) there is; we have, فيه, [feeh] 8
Djibouti, جيبوتي, [jeebootee], Pre-Lesson
doctor (m), طَبيب / أطِبّاء, [Tabeeb/aTibbaa'], 6
dollar, دولار / ـات, [doolaar /--aat], 2
driver, سائِق / ـين, [saa'iq/--een], 4
duration, مُدّة, [muddah], 8
Egypt, مِصْر, [miSr], Pre-Lesson
Egyptian (m), مِصْري, [miSree], 1
engineer (f), مُهَنْدِسة / ـات, [muhandisah/--aat], 6
engineer (m), مُهَنْدِس / ـين, [muhandis/--een], 6
Enjoy your meal!, !بالصِّحّة, [biS-SaHHah], 8
every, كُلّ, [kull], 2
everything, كُلّ شَيْء, [kull shay'], 1
excellent, عَظيم, ['aTheem], 5

Glossary

excuse me, لَوْ سَمَحْت, [law samaHt], 4
expensive, غالي, [ghaalee], 7
extended family, عائلة / ـات, ['aailah/--aat], 6
fabric, قُماش / أقْمِشة, [qumaash/aqmishah], 7
far, بعيد, [ba'eed], 3
fasting person, صائم / ـين, [Saa'im/--een], 9
father, أب / آباء, [ab/aaba'], 9
feast celebrating end of Ramadan, عيد الفِطْر, ['eed al-fiTr], 9
feast day, عيد / أعْياد, ['eed/a'yaad], 9
fifty, خمسين, [khamseen], 3
film, فيلم / أفْلام, [feelm/aflaam], 6
film director (m), مُخرِج / ـين, [mukhrij/--een], 6
food; meal, أكْل / ـات, [akl/--aat], 8
for an hour, لِمُدَّة ساعة, [limuddat saa'ah], 8
for you (f), لَكِ, [laki], 7
for you (m), لَكَ, [laka], 7
for, in order to, لِ, [li], 7
form, shape, شَكْل / أشْكال, [shakl/ashkaal], 7
freeway, أُوتُسْتْراد, [utoostraad], 4
friend, صديق / أصْدِقاء, [Sadeeq/aSdiqaa'], 5
friendly; nice, لطيف / لُطَفاء, [laTeef/luTafaa'], 4
from, مِن, [min], 1
from here; this way, مِن هُنا, [min hunaa], 3
from where, مِن أيْن, [min ayna], 1
fruit, فواكِه, [fawaakih], 8
full, شَبْعان / ـين, [shab'aan/--een], 9
garden, حديقة / حدائق, [Hadeeqah/Hidaa'iq], 2
generous, كريم / كِرام, [kareem/kiraam], 9
girl; daughter, بِنْت / بنات (f), [bint/banaat], 6
give (m) me, أعْطِني, [a'Tinee], 2
glass, كأس / كُؤوس, [ka's/ku'oos], 8
God (is my witness)!, واللهِ!, [wa allaah], 6
God willing; hopefully, إن شاء الله, [inshaa' allaah], 1
gold, ذهب, [thahab], 7
good, تَمام, [tamaam], 1
good, جيّد / ـين, [jayyid/--een], 7
good; good-natured, طيّب / ـين, [Tayyib/--een], 4
good; OK, طيِّب, [Tayyib], 2
great, super, مُمْتاز, [mumtaaz], 4
greetings to you., تحيّة طيّبة وبعد, [taHeeyah Tayyibah wa-ba'ad], 5
(phrase to begin a letter)
greeting, تَحِيّة / ـات, [taHayyah/--aat], 9
guys! (informal), يا شباب!, [yaa shabaab], 6
half, نِصْف, [niSf], 5
handmade, يدوي, [yadawee], 7
have (m) a seat!, إجْلِس!, [ijlis], 7
have a pleasant stay! (lit. a happy stay), إقامة سعيدة!, [iqaamah sa'eedah], 2

heart, قَلْب, [qalb], 2
hello! (on the phone), آلو, [aaloo], 5
here, هُنا, [hunaa], 3
Here (you go), تَفَضَّل, [tafaDDal], 2
here you (pl) are, تفضَّلوا, [tafaDDaloo], 8
Hi! (lit. Be a relative), أهلاً, [ahlan], 1
hi; A warm welcome, أهلاً وسهلاً, [ahlan wa sahlan], 1
high, عالي, ['aalee], 7
hotel, فُندُق / فنادِق, [funduq/fanaadiq], 2
hour; clock, ساعة / ـات, [saa'ah/--aat], 5
how, كيْف, [kayfa], 1
How about?, ما رأيك (بـ), [maa ra'yak (bi)], 3
How are you?, كيْف الأحْوال؟, [kayf al-aHwaal], 6
How are you?, كيْف الحال؟, [kayfa al-Haal], 1
How are you (m)? (lit. What's your condition?), كيْف حالك؟, [kayfa Haalak], 1
how many, كَم, [kam], 2
how many nights? (lit. How many night?), كَم ليلة؟, [kam laylah], 2
how much, بكم, [bi-kam], 2
how old are they?, كَم عُمرُهُم؟, [kam 'umruhum], 6
how's the family?, كيْف العائلة؟, [kayf al-'aailah], 6
hungry, جوعان / ـين, [jaw'aan/--een], 8
Hurghada (resort town), الغَرْدَقة, [al-ghardaqah], 6
I, أنا, [anā], 1
I called you (f), اتَّصلت بكِ, ['itaSalt biki], 5
I hope (that) ..., أتَمَنّى أنْ ..., [atamannaa an...], 9
I like/love, أحِبّ, [uHibb], 1
I love, أحِبّ, ['uHibb], 5
I study/learn, أدْرُس, [adrus], 1
I understood, فَهِمت, [fahimt], 2
I'm sorry., أنا آسف (ـة), [anaa aasif (ah)], 5
I'm sorry (for), أنا آسف (على), [anaa aasif ('alaa)], 8
I'm sorry; allow (m) me, لَوْ سَمَحْت, [law samaHt], 3
idea, فِكرة / أفْكار, [fikrah / afkaar], 8
I'll take, آخُذ, [aakhuth], 2
impossible, مُسْتَحيل, [mustaHeel], 7
In, في, [fee], 1
in addition, بالإضافة إلى ذلك, [bil-iDaafah ilaa thaalik], 7
in the afternoon, بعد الظُّهر, [b'ad aTH-Thuhr], 5
in the evening, في المساء, [fee al-masaa'], 5
in the morning, في الصَّباح, [fi asS-SabaaH], 5
in the name of God, بِسْم الله, [bis-mil-laah], 9
instant; moment, لحظة / ـات, [laHTHah/--aat], 2
international, عالمي / ـين, ['aalamee/--een], 6
Iraq, العِراق, [al-'iraaq], **Pre-Lesson**
it (f) is not, ليْست, [laysat], 4
it was my pleasure, فُرْصة سَعيدة, [furSah sa'eedah], 1
goodbye, مَع السَّلامة, [ma' as-salaamah], 1

Glossary

dan, الأُرْدُنّ [al-urdunn], **Pre-Lesson**
ce, عَصير [ʻaSeer], 8
y, مِفتاح / مَفاتيح [miftaaH/mafaateeH], 2
wait, الكُوَيْت [al-kuwayt], **Pre-Lesson**
guage, لُغة [lughah], 1
ge; big, كَبير / كِبار [kabeer kibaar], 3
f, وَرَق / أَوْراق [waraq/awraaq], 8
anon, لُبنان [lubnaan], **Pre-Lesson**
ons, لَيْمون [laymoon], 8
tils, عَدَس [ʻadiss], 8
s (adv), قَليلاً [qaliilan], 6
ter, رِسالة / رَسائل [risaalah/rasaaʼil], 5
tuce, خَسّ [khass], 8
ya, ليبيا [leebiyaa], **Pre-Lesson**
; age, عُمْر [ʻumr], 6
a (Syr. pound), لَيْرة / ات [layrah/--aat], 7
le, صَغير / صِغار [Sagheer/Sighaar], 3
tle, قَليل / ين [qaleel/--een], 7
ve, حُبّ [Hubb], 6
any thanks, أَلْف شُكر [alf shukr], 3
ap, خَريطة [khareeTah], 3
arket, سوق / أَسْواق (f) [sooq/aswaaq], 3
arried, مُتَزَوِّج / ين [mutazawwij/--een], 6
auritania, موريتانيا [mooreetaanyaa], **Pre-Lesson**
easurement, مِقْدار / مَقادير [miqdaar/maqaadeer], 8
edicine, طِبّ [Tibb], 9
eters, مِتْر / أَمْتار [mitir/amtaar], 3
ilitarily, عَسْكَري [ʻaskaree], 4
int, نَعْناع [naʻnaaʻ], 8
inute, دَقيقة / دَقائِق [daqeeqah/daqaaʼiq], 5
orocco, المَغْرِب [al-maghrib], **Pre-Lesson**
osaic, موزاييك [muzaayeek], 7
osque, جامِع / جَوامِع [jamiʻ/jawaamiʻ], 3
other, أُمّ / أُمَّهات (f) [umm/ummahaat], 9
r., سَيِّد / سادة [sayyid / saadah], 2
uch, كَثير / ين [katheer/--een], 5
useum, مَتْحَف / مَتاحِف [matHaf/mataaHif], 3
y dear (f) (address in private letters), عَزيزَتي [ʻazeezatee], 5
y friends, أَصْدِقائي [aSdiqaaʼee], 1
y name is, اِسْمي [ismee], 1
y pleasure (lit. we are honored), تَشَرَّفْنا [tasharrafnaa], 1
ame, اِسْم [ism], 1
ational, وَطَني / ين [waTanee/--een], 3
ationality, جِنْسِيّة [jinseeyah], 1
ear; nearby, قَريب [qareeb], 3
ew, جَديد / جُدُد [jadeed/judud], 3

next to, جَنْب [janb], 3
night, لَيْلة / لَيالي [laylah/layaalee], 2
no, لا [laa], 1
now, الآن [al-aan], 5
occasion, مُناسَبة / ات [munaasabah/--aat], 9
of course, طَبْعاً [Tabʻan], 2
of course, طَبْعاً [Tabʻan], 4
office, مَكْتَب / مَكاتِب [maktab/makaatib], 5
oil, زَيْت [zayt], 8
old, قَديم / قُدَماء [qadeem/qudamaaʼ], 3
olives, زَيْتون [zaytoon], 8
Oman, عُمان [ʻumaan], **Pre-Lesson**
on, على [ʻalaa], 2
on the right, عَلى اليَمين [ʻalaa al-yameen], 3
one, واحِد [waaHid], 2
one hundred percent, مائة بالمائة [maaʼah bi-l-maaʼh], 3
onions, بَصَل [baSal], 8
only, فَقَط [faqaT], 7
or, أَوْ [aw], 7
oriental; Middle Eastern, شَرْقي / ين [sharqee/--een], 5
Palestine, فَلَسْطين [filasTeen], **Pre-Lesson**
Palestinian (f), فَلَسْطينِيّة [filasTeeneeyah], 1
parsley, بَقْدونِس [baqdoonis], 8
passport, جَواز / ات [jawaaz /--aat], 2
people, ناس [naas], 4
photographing, تَصْوير [taSweer], 4
piece, حَبّة [Habbah], 8
place of birth, مَكان الميلاد [makaan al-meelaad], 1
plate, صَحْن / صُحون [SaHin/SuHoon], 8
please (f), مِن فَضْلِك [min faDlak], 2
please (m), مِن فَضْلَك [min faDlak], 2
possible; one can مُمْكِن [mumkin] 7
preparation, طَريقة [Tareeqah], 8
present, gift, هَدِيّة / هَدايا [hadeeyah/hadaayaa], 7
price, سِعْر / أَسْعار [siʻr/asʻaar], 7
problem مُشْكِلة / مَشاكِل [mushkilah/mashaakil] 6
product, مَصْنوع / ات [munṭajʻ/--aat], 7
professor; master, أُسْتاذ / أَساتِذة [ustaath/asaatithah], 7
prohibited, مَمْنوع [mamnooʻ], 4
pyramid, هَرَم / أَهْرام [haram/ahraam], 5
Qatar, قَطَر [qaTar], **Pre-Lesson**
quality, جَوْدة [jawdah], 7
Ramadan, رَمَضان [ramaDaan], 9
rarity, تُحْفة / تُحَف [tuHfah/tuHaf], 7
really, فِعْلاً [fiʻlan], 7
red (f), حَمْراء [Hamraaʼ], 7
reduce! (lit. make easier), خَفِّف [khaffif], 4

Glossary

response to God bless you, الله يُبارك فيك, [allaah ybaarik feek], 7
restaurant, مَطْعَم / مَطَاعِم, [maT'am/maTaa'im], 2
rice, رُزّ, [ruzz], 8
right away; at once, فَوْراً, [fawran], 6
room, غُرْفَة / غُرَف, [ghurfah/ghuraf], 2
safety, أَمان, [amaan], 4
salad, سلطة / ـات, [salaTah/--aat], 8
salt, مِلْح, [milH], 8
Saudi Arabia, اَلسَّعودية, [as-sa'oodeeyah], Pre-Lesson
say! (f), قولي, [qoolee], 9
sea, بَحْر, [baHr], 2
see you later (lit. until meeting), إلى اللِّقاء, [ilaa al-liqaa'], 1
seven, سَبْعة, [sab'ah], 2
shortly afterwards (lit. after little), بَعْد قَليل, [ba'd qaleel], 3
sick, مَريض, [mareeD], 6
sign, إشارة, [ishaarah], 4
silver, فِضّة, [fiDDah], 7
simple, easy, سَهْل, [sahl], 4
since, مُنْذُ, [munthu], 3
sincere; honest, مُخْلِص / ـين, [mukhliS/--een], 9
sister, أُخْت / أَخَوات (f), [ukht/akhawaat], 9
Somalia, الصومال, [aS-Soomaal], Pre-Lesson
son, اِبْن / أَبْناء, [ibn/abnaa'], 6
souk al-Hamidiya, سوق الحميدية, [sooq al-Hameedeeyah], 7
soup, شوربة, [shoorbah], 8
speed, سُرْعة, [sur'ah], 4
spoon, مِلْعَقة / مَلاعِق, [mil'aqah/malaa'iq], 8
square, ساحة / ـات, [saaHah/--aat], 3
Stop!, قِف, [qif], 4
store, shop, مَحَلّ / ـات, [maHall/--aat], 7
story, قِصّة, [qiSSah], 6
straight ahead, عَلى طول, ['aala Tool], 3
over there, هُناك, [hunaak], 3
street, شارِع / شَوارِع, [shaari'/shawaari'], 3
Sudan, السودان, [as-sudaan], Pre-Lesson
sugar, سُكَّر, [sukkar], 7
sweets, حلويّات, [Halaweeyaat], 9
Syria, سوريا, [sooriyaa], Pre-Lesson
Syrian (f), سوريّة, [sooreeyah], 1
tabbouleh (salad with a lot of parsley), تبّولة, [tabboolih], 8
take (m)!/get (m)!, خُذ!, [khuth], 7
taxi, تاكْسي / تَكاسي, [taaksee/takaasee], 4
taxi meter, عَدّاد, ['adaad], 4
tea, شاي, [shaay], 5
telephone, تليفون, [tileefoon], 5
thank God (lit. God be praised), الحَمْدُ لله, [al-Hamdu lil-laah], 1
thank you very much, شُكْراً جَزيلاً, [shukran jazeelan], 1

thank you very much, شُكْراً جَزيلاً, [shukran jazeelan], 2
that you (m), إنَّك, [innaka], 9
the first minute, اَلدَّقيقة الأُولى, [ad-daqeeqah al-'oolaa], 5
the left, اليَسار, [al-yasaar], 3
The Orient, شَرْقيّات, [sharqeeyaat], 7
then, ثُمَّ, [thumma], 8
then, ثُمّ, [thumm], 6
these are; these (pl with persons), هَؤُلاء, [haa'ulaa'], 1
thing; something, شَيء / أَشْياء, [shay'/ashyaa'], 5
thirsty, عَطْشان / ـين, ['aTshaan/--een], 9
This (is) on me., الحِساب عَلَيَّ, [al-Hisaab 'alayya], 8
this is; this (f), هَذِهِ, [haathihi], 1
this is; this (m), هَذا, [haathaa], 1
this time, هَذِه المَرَّة, [haathihi al-marrah], 8
three, ثَلاثة, [thalaathaa], 3
time, وَقْت / أَوْقات, [waqt/awqaat], 5
to, إلى, [ilaa], 3
to add, أَضاف ـ يُضيف (إلى) IV, [aDaaf -- yuDeef (ilaa)], 8
to arrive, وَصَل ـ يَصِل, [waSal -- yaSil], 9
to ask (for), سَأَل ـ يَسْأَل (عن), [sa'al -- yas'al ('an)], 7
to begin; to start, بَدَأَ ـ يَبْدَأ, [bada' -- yabda'], 9
to begin; to start, بَدَأَ ـ يَبْدَأ, [bada' -- yabda'], 6
to bring, أَحْضَر ـ يُحْضِر IV, [aHDar -- yuHDir], 8
to buy, اِشْتَرى, ['ishtaraa], 5
to buy, اِشْتَرى ـ يَشْتَري, [ishtaraa -- yashtaree], 7
to cook, طَبَخ ـ يَطْبُخ, [Tabakh -- yaTbukh], 9
to cut, قَطَع ـ يَقْطَع, [qaTa' -- yaqTa'], 8
to do; to make, فَعَل, [fa'al], 5
to drain, صَفّى ـ يُصَفّي, [Saffaa -- yuSaffee], 8
to drink, شَرِب, [sharib], 5
to drink, شَرِب ـ يَشْرَب, [sharib -- yashrab], 6
to eat, أَكَل ـ يَأْكُل, [akal -- ya'kul], 8
to enter; to come in, دَخَل ـ يَدْخُل, [dakhal -- yadkhul], 9
to fall, وَقَع ـ يَقَع, [waqa' -- yaqa'], 6
to fall in love, وَقَع في الحُبّ, [waqa' fee al-Hubb], 6
to find, وَجَد ـ يَجِد, [wajad -- yajid], 7
to give, أَعْطى ـ يُعْطي VI, [a'Taa -- yu'Tee], 9
to go, ذَهَب ـ يَذْهَب, [thahab -- yathhab], 6
to go, to walk, ذَهَب, [thahab], 5
to hope, تَمَنَّى ـ يتمنَّى V, [tamannaa -- yatamannaa], 9
to know; to find out, عَرَف ـ يَعْرِف, ['arif - ya'rif], 6
to learn, to study, دَرَس ـ يَدْرُس, [dars -- yadrus], 6
to like (to do), أَراد ـ يُريد أَن (يَفْعل) VI, [araad -- yureed an (yaf'al)], 9
to like, to love, أَحَبَّ ـ يُحِبّ IV, [aHabb -- yuHibb], 8
to like, to want, أَراد ـ يُريد IV, [araad -- yureed], 8
to live; to reside, سَكَن ـ يَسْكُن, [sakan -- yaskun], 6
to look (for), بَحَث ـ يَبْحَث (عن), [baHath – yabHath ('an)], 7

Glossary

make, عمل – يعْمل, ['amil -- ya'mal], 7
meet, قابل – يُقابل, [qaabal -- yuqaabil], 6
need, احْتاج – يحْتاج (إلى), [iHtaaj -- yaHtaaj (ilaa)], 7
order, طلب – يطْلب, [Talab -- yaTlub], 8
pay, دفع – يدْفع, [dafa' -- yadfa'], 7
prefer, II فضّل – يُفضّل, [faDDal -- yufaDDil], 8
present, قدّم – يُقدّم (لـ), [qaddam – yuqaddim (li)], 7
put, وضع – يضع, [waDa' -- yaDa'], 8
return (to), رجع – يرْجع (إلى), [raja' -- yarji' (ilaa)], 9
say (to s.o.), قال – يقول (لـ), [qaal – yaqool (li)], 9
say that ..., قال إنّ ..., [qaal inna...], 9
see, رأى – يرى, [ra'aa -- yaraa], 6
send (to), VI أرْسل – يُرْسل (إلى), [arsal -- yursil (ilaa)], 9
serve بهارات [bihaaraat] 8
sit, جلس – يجْلس, [jalas -- yajlis], 6
soak, نقع – ينْقع, [naqa' -- yanqa'], 8
speak, تكلّم – يتكلّم, [takallam -- yatakallam], 6
take, أخذ – يأْخذ, [akhath-ya'khuth], 7
telephone, to call, اتّصل (بـ), ['itaSal (bi)], 5
understand, فهم – يفْهم, [fahim -- yafham], 6
visit, زار – يزور, [zaar -- yazoor], 9
wait (for), VIII انْتظر – ينْتظر, [intaThar -- yantaThir], 8
walk out (of), خرج – يخْرج (من), [kharaj -- yakhruj (min)], 9
wash, غسل – يغْسل, [ghasal -- yaghsil], 8
work, اشْتغل – يشْتغل, [ishtaghal -- yashtaghil], 6
write, كتب, [katab], 5
day, اليوم, [al-yawm], 5
matoes, طماطم, [TamaaTim], 8
morrow, غداً, [ghadan], 5
morrow (lit. the day tomorrow), يوم الغد, [yawm al-ghad], 5
ur, جوْلة / ـات, [jawlah/--aat], 3
wn, مدينة / مدن, [madeenah/mudun], 2
affic, مرور, [muroor], 4
ain, قطار / ـات, [qiTaar /--aat], 4
ain station; stop, محطّة / ـات, [maHaTTah/--aat], 3
nisia, تونس, [toonis], Pre-Lesson
cle, عمّ, ['amm], 9
nited Arab Emirates (UAE), الإمارات, [al-imaaraat], Pre-Lesson
nited Arabic Emirates (UAE), الإمارات, [al-imaaraat], 4
egetables, خضر, [khuDar], 8
ery, جدّاً, [jiddan], 4
aiter, جرْسون, [jarsoon], 8
ater, ماء, [maa'], 8
ater pipe, (hockah) نرْجيلة / ـات, [narjeelah/--aat], 7
ay; road; route, طريق / طُرُق, [Tareeq/Turuq], 3
e, نحْنُ, [naHnu], 1
e are not, لسْنا, [lasnaa], 4

we present you, نُقدّم لكم, [nuqaddam lakum], 7
week, أسْبوع / أسابيع, ['usboo'/asaabee'], 2
well, جيّداً, [jayyidan], 1
well/good (lit. with kindness), بخيْر, [bi-khayr], 1
what, ما, [maa], 1
what is God's will! (expression of admiration), ما شاء الله !, [maa shaa' allaah!], 6
what (in questions with verbs), ماذا, [maathaa], 5
what time is it? (lit. How much is the hour?), كم الساعة ؟, [kam as-saa'ah], 5
what's that in Arabic?, ما اسْمه بالعربي ؟, [maa ismuh bi-l-'arabee], 2
what's your (f) name?, ما اسْمك ؟, [maa ismik], 1
what's your (m) name?, ما اسْمك ؟, [maa ismak], 1
What's your opinion about, ما رأيك (بـ), [maa ra'yak (bi)], 4
where, أيْن, ['ayna], 3
which, أيّ, [ayy], 5
who, مَن, [man], 6
who is this?, مَن هذا ؟, [man haathaa], 6
who's there? (lit. Who's with me?), من معي ؟, [man ma'ee], 5
wife, زوْجة, [zawjah], 6
with, مع, [ma'], 7
with me, معي, [ma'ee], 3
with pleasure, بكلّ سرور, [bi-kull suroor], 5
with pleasure (lit. with every joy), بكلّ سرور, [bi-kull suroor], 3
with; in, بـ, [bi], 2
woman; lady; ma'am, سيّدة / ـات, [sayyidah/--aat], 3
year, سنة / سنوات, [sanah/sanawaat], 4
yellow, (f) صفْراء, [Safraa'], 7
Yemen, اليمن, [al-yaman], Pre-Lesson
Yes, نعم, [na'am], 1
yesterday, أمس, [ams], 5
you (f) (lit. your (f) presence), حضْرتك, [HaDritik], 5
you (f) are not, لسْت, [lasti], 4
you (inform) speak, تتكلّم, [tatakallam], 1
you (m) (lit. your (m) presence), حضْرتك, [HaDritak], 4
you (m) are not, لسْت, [lasta], 4
you (m) know, تعْرف, [ta'rif], 3
you (m) were; I was, كنْت, [kunt], 4
you (m, sing), أنْت, [anta], 1
you (pl), أنْتم, [antum], 1
young man, (pl:) youth, شاب / شباب, [shaab/shabaab], 6
you're welcome!/Excuse me?, عفْواً, ['afwan], 2

143